LABOR
INTO
ART

LABOR INTO ART

The Theme of Work in Nineteenth-Century American Literature

David Sprague Herreshoff

Wayne State University Press   Detroit

Manufactured in the United States of America.
95 94 93 92 91 5 4 3 2 1

**Library of Congress
Cataloging-in-Publication Data**

Herreshoff, David Sprague, 1921–
Labor into art : the theme of work in nineteenth-century American literature / David Sprague Herreshoff.
p. cm.
Includes bibliographical references and index.
ISBN 0–8143–2081–3 (alk. paper)
1. American literature—19th century—History and criticism. 2. Working class in literature. 3. Work in literature. I. Title.
PS217.W66H4 1991
810.9′355′09034—dc20 90–20754
CIP

The book was designed by Mary Primeau.

To the Scottish Calvinist overseer
who exacted this labor

Who first invented work?

—Charles Lamb

The degradation of work through the division of labor is not in the world Edward Taylor represents in God's Determinations Touching His Elect*—Taylor's Creative Worker uses carpentry, metallurgy and foundry work, stonemasonry, and housewifery. Taylor's God is no drudging specialist but truly a master of all trades. Emily Dickinson imagines God as a production manager who lets angels out to play in the afternoons if they have met their daily work quota. Between the seventeenth and nineteenth centuries God declined from a master craftsman into a mere supervisor, if the witness of Taylor and Dickinson can be credited.*

—David Herreshoff

CONTENTS

INTRODUCTION

American writers who matured in the mid-nineteenth century store our memories with the perceptions of the generation that experienced the beginning of their nation's economic dominance and cultural independence. When engaged with the theme of work, their poetry, essays, and fiction penetrate and judge what making a living felt like as they took in and imagined the experience. I try to see in this study what five of them make of the theme of work. The five are Henry David Thoreau, Herman Melville, Emily Dickinson, Frederick Douglass, and Walt Whitman.

Lodged in the productions of these five authors are responses to questions they wrestled with in their workaday lives. What, they asked, is the connection between how one makes a living and one's character? How do men and women endure oppressive or celebrate liberating work experiences? Is the line between work and leisure always clear? What is the relation between the work done and the leisure enjoyed by a person? Is the work experience primarily fraternal and cooperative or despotic and hierarchical, sociable or isolating, punitive or redemptive, enslaving or liberating?

This cluster of questions may be grouped under a basic, organizing question: What does work do to human beings? And to this basic question another may be linked, which the five writers respond to in their creative practice: How may what work does to people become matter for literature? The answers of the five are those of an essayist who drew on his experiences as a house builder and gardener, of a novelist whose memory of life as a seaman fed his creativity, of a poet who doubled as a housekeeper and made poetry from drudgery, of a field and house slave who made psychodrama of the struggle to be free, and of a jack of several trades and master of the bardic tradition who sought to cheer up slaves and horrify despots. Each of these five learned how to use inevitable economic routines to keep literature alive.

What I see in these authors is conditioned by where I stand. Time spent in factories and universities in quests for peace and justice and a long-held conviction that workers can change the world for the better surely affect my interpretations. So also does an idea I received from Marx through Trotsky—though not requiring their endorsement—that you do not have to like a writer's politics to admire a writer's art. Whether my standpoint confers on me the label "Marxist" I will leave to others. Marxism has become a house with many mansions and even outhouses. I would be willing to be numbered among the residents of some of these quarters but not of others. If to be a Marxist requires believing that criticism is the master and not the servant of literature and that books write themselves and are self-referential, I am not a Marxist. For me the human subject laboring to transform the world is still to be reckoned with. So also are authors wrestling with their cultural inheritance and situation. Not only do I believe that they lived in history and changed literature, I also take delight in what they created. If I take some of those creations apart it is not because I think I can improve on their construction.

The long association of literature with leisure classes exempt from the need to provide themselves with food, shelter, and clothing produces a representation of human experience in literature that ignores, neglects, or patronizes people at work. Thoreau notes in "Life without Principle" that

> there is little or nothing to be remembered written on the subject of getting a living; how to make getting a living not merely honest and honorable, but altogether inviting and glorious; for if *getting* a living is not so, then living is not. One would think, from looking at literature, that the question never disturbed a solitary individual's musings. Is it that men are too disgusted with their experience to speak of it? (*NA,* 1756)[1]

When he wrote this Thoreau had decisively broken with the idea that work is a disgusting subject for a writer and better avoided than dwelt on. He wrote memorably in *Walden* on getting a living. He develops there his understanding that the quality of life is dependent on how one makes a living and that the study of work is the study of culture. And since culture changes through time, *Walden* is in part a report on Thoreau's experimental reenactment of transitional events in economic history. In the weight he gives to that history, Thoreau is more of a historical materialist than one might suppose a transcendentalist ought to be. Sometimes the line between transcendent idealism and materialism seems scarcely visible. On the importance of economic history the thoughts of Thoreau and Marx are close. In 1844, the year before Thoreau went to live at Walden Pond, Marx was thinking about the history of industry. He calls it "the open book of man's essential powers, the exposure to the senses of human psychology."[2]

If what Marx says about the history of industry is true, being mindful of that history can enrich and complicate our understanding of literature. To use Marx's assumption as an aid to literary criticism the reader must grant, provisionally at least, that history is shaped more by conflicts between groups of people who get their livings in different ways—in other words, by class struggles—than it is by conflicts between men and women, between parents and children, between siblings, between nations or tribes, or between the gods and humankind. Applying this assumption should help locate and interpret representations of the work experience in literature overlooked or slighted in readings governed by other assumptions about the world. Taking Marx's idea about the instructiveness of the history of industry seriously does not require a reader to ignore or deny that there is much in the vision of writers having little or nothing to do with class. Tolerant pluralism ought to prevail in the republic of letters, I believe, if criticism is to contribute to the shaping of a culture in which the achievements of prehistoric, ancient, feudal, and bourgeois thought and art are readily accessible, a culture that will keep alive the vision of a society in which the split between the commanders and the commanded has been overcome and the free development of each is a condition for the free development of all.

What does work do to human beings? To look for answers suggested by the five writers is to come upon complex, variable, and sometimes evasive responses. But the answers that scrutiny of the writing yields share at least one fundamental thought: the division of labor produces a fragmentation of personality. Marx shares this thought with the American writers of his generation. The criticism of work in that generation is associated with a tacit or articulate utopianism that judges the capitalist present by the standard of a past or future world. In Marx's version, with the appearance of the division of labor

> each man has a particular, exclusive sphere of activity, which is forced upon him and from which he cannot escape. He is a hunter, a fisherman, a shepherd, or a critical critic, and must remain so if he is not to lose his means of livelihood; while in a communist society, where nobody has one exclusive sphere of activity, but each one can become accomplished in any branch he wishes, society regulates the general production and thus makes it possible for me to do one thing today and another tomorrow, to hunt in the morning, fish in the afternoon, rear cattle in the evening, criticize after dinner, just as I have in mind, without ever becoming hunter, fisherman, shepherd or critic.[3]

Not to be merely what you do and to have the sentence of life under the division of labor commuted become defining traits of the utopian kingdom of freedom. When Marx criticizes the division of labor from the standpoint of an unalienating, because variegated, mode of production, he does not differ substantially from Ralph Waldo Emerson in a passage of "The American Scholar" where Man Thinking is counterposed to the Thinker and Man on the Farm to the Farmer. In Emerson the labor process in modern society chops people up "into so many walking monsters—a good finger, a neck, a stomach, but never a man." Characterizing individuals by the work they do, society degrades everyone from subject to object:

> Man is thus metamorphosed into a thing. The planter . . . sinks into a farmer instead of man on the farm. The tradesman . . . is ridden by the routine of his craft and the soul is subject to dollars. The priest becomes a form; . . . the mechanic a machine; the sailor a rope of the ship. . . . Man Thinking tends to become a mere thinker, or still worse, the parrot of other men's thinking. (*NA,* 694)

When they protest what work does to workers and a society that types people according to their occupations while restricting them to a single occupation, Marx and Emerson are optimists. For both, the condition protested is historical, not eternal; it did not always exist and will not always exist. The human fall from subject to object, from freedom to servitude embodied in the division of labor and private property is, for Marx, a "consolidation of what we ourselves produce into an objective power above us, growing out of our control, thwarting our expectations, bringing to naught our calculations."[4] Their accounts of alienation entitle Emerson and Marx to be listed among the heirs of Old Testament prophets like Isaiah who inveigh against the idolatry that compels human beings to subordinate themselves to the products of their own hands. The revolutionary longing for a leap from the kingdom of necessity into the kingdom of freedom descends from the same source.

Although Thoreau complains in "Life without Principle" about the absence from literature of the theme of getting a living, writers sharing his interest in the literary representation of work are plentiful. The four writers who with Thoreau are subjects of this study are notable examples. Herman Melville, for one, saw the fragmentation of humanity when he formed his vision of what happens to workers by experience aboard the floating factory he went to sea in in 1841 and indirectly as a witness to the industrial revolution on shore. Melville would not have known Marx's account of the division of labor in *The German Ideology* but would have been familiar with Emerson's description of it in "The American Scholar." But because Marx and Emerson agree pretty well on the topic and because Melville's view is close to theirs, one can see in *Moby-Dick* a meditation on what Marx calls that "consolidation of what we ourselves produce into an objective power over us, growing out of our control," or, alternately, as a demonstration of the process in which, according to Emerson, "the sailor becomes a rope of the ship." Nineteenth-century optimists like Emerson and Marx hope that the recognition of necessity can give rise to chances for human freedom. Pessimists, and Melville was one, see unmanageable doom in the course of history. The recognition of alienation is the foundation for revolt or despair or both.

There is a dialectical interdependence between character and fate, personality and occupation, in the writers I study here. In them the work experience confirms and illumines some characters and transforms others. Less often do the internal powers and will of a character transform work. Thoreau is the chief exemplar of that cheerful option. For Emily Dickinson, by contrast, work is usually something to be endured or escaped from. When they improvise on the theme of work, Thoreau and Dickinson are concerned with outdoor and indoor labor respectively. To turn from Thoreau to Dickinson—in examples of their writing where they draw imagery from work and its results—is to turn from a house builder to a housekeeper. There are exceptions to this generalization. Thoreau has thoughts about housekeeping, which range from irritation with himself for keeping something unnecessary in his cabin that requires dusting, to the wish to reduce the store of provisions to the point where rodents will no longer be baited into the cabin, to arguing for a vegetarian diet because cleaning fish and game and cleaning up afterward are a messy waste of time. Thoreau's slogan is nothing for housekeeping. Thoreau's cabin is mainly a shelter from which to range toward the woods or toward the village—a frontier situation with nature and civilization equally accessible; it is also a writer's study. The building of his cabin is an opportunity to meditate on the work experience and the condition of the laborer, both in and out of nature.

Dickinson, to concede another exception, has plenty of open-air poems. In them she is almost always an observer who has put housekeeping out of her mind. An intriguing variation is in Poem 219 in which the landscape is a house and Nature is personified as a sloppy housekeeper.[5] The inhabitants of other Dickinson nature poems enjoy a world where the split between work and play does not exist and where drudgery is consequently unknown. It is an attractive world, sadly inaccessible to humanity. The drudging aspect of housekeeping is the most usual source of Dickinson's work imagery. In her poems of this sort work is a solitary and sometimes thankfully benumbing recourse of a tortured spirit.

The drudgery of forced labor and its effects on character make an important theme for Frederick Douglass. In contrast to Thoreau and Dickinson, Douglass's focus is on social, not solitary, work experience. Douglass's account of work is conditioned by a rhetorical purpose not shared by the other four writers. The purpose of a narrative such as Douglass's is to convince an audience of nonslaves of the intolerable because dehumanizing consequences of slave labor. Douglass's telling of his life as a slave is organized around a psychological crisis giving rise to his self-emancipation from servility. At first he internalizes the master-slave relation, convinced that what is, is right. Then he rebels and ceases to be a slave in spirit before he ceases to be a slave in the flesh. (A like self-emancipation occurs in Melville's Ishmael—the only mariner aboard the *Pequod* who renounces his allegiance to the despotic commander.) Douglass knows that to sway his audience he must deliver a plausible description of slavery. This he does by individualizing characters. Not all masters are alike and not all slaves. And different masters and slaves change, for the better or for the worse.

Much of the time Walt Whitman is a perfunctory praiser of work but an entirely inspired celebrator of lolling and loafing in the grass. When he celebrates work, it is likely to be work as it might be in a utopian future rather than work as it is. Where Dickinson longs for a condition of work beyond human reach and to be seen only in the instinctive, spontaneous activity of birds and insects, Whitman focuses on possibilities latent or emergent in humanity. Millenarian optimism weakens the sense of ugly present reality in him and almost expunges traces of satire from his announcements and celebrations of what is to be. Describing work, he is more interested in the process, with its display of human powers and its occasions for comradeship, than he is in the product of work. Whitman is amused by work and compassionate toward those engaged in it. His amusement is allied to conviction that work can be reunited with play. His celebration of work expresses a prophetic faith that when the product is no longer expropriated from the producers, work will be accompanied by song: the production of worldly and spiritual goods will go on together. Still, the makers and the making will remain more important than what is made. Whitman sanctifies work like his Puritan antecedents, for whom to work was to pray. Work, like leisure, becomes for Whitman a way of knowing the world.

1.

What Thoreau Made of His House

WALDEN MAY BE READ for its account of one man's attempt to work as efficiently, independently, and as little as is compatible with health, recording an attempt to find in work a means to knowledge about the world and the self. Read this way, the focus of the book's attention is on the integration of work and leisure with the cycle of the seasons as a way of meeting the material, emotional, and intellectual needs of a human being. Thoreau in *Walden* often links his consideration of the theme of work with the experience of building his cabin, but he has much to say about the work experience of others from prehistoric times to his own. Not wishing to impose a dogmatic, how-to tract on his readers, he nevertheless invites them to consider whether his experience, researches, and conclusions might benefit them. Such a reading may draw attention to facets of *Walden* that are glimpsed only askance, if at all, in other readings.

Thoreau's appraisal of work is both subjective and objective. His primary concern is with the worker as feeling, thinking actor in nature and history. He will not appraise the product (the object of labor) without first inquiring what making the product did to the worker (the laboring subject). He tests on his own muscles, nerves, and mind the limits beyond which the humanizing experience of work becomes the dehumanizing experience of labor. The test question he asks of work experience is: does it make the worker more or less human, does it cost more than it comes to?

Two examples, one from his own time and one from antiquity, will illustrate his procedure. The quality of a product of labor directly expresses the conditions and motives of the mode of production for Thoreau when he writes:

> I cannot believe that our factory system is the best mode by which men may get their clothing. The condition of the operatives is becoming every day more like that of the English; and it cannot be wondered at, since, as far as I have heard or observed, the principal object is, not that mankind may be well and decently clothed, but unquestionably, that the corporations may be enriched. In the long run men hit only what they aim at. (*NA*, 1547)

For Thoreau the degradation of the producers and the shoddy degeneration of the product are complementary structural elements of capitalism. He protests the condition of the workers before protesting the quality of what they make because their condition is more important to him. Visible in this passage is Thoreau's belief that meeting material human needs is the just end of working and that this end cannot be justified if the means to it degrade the workers.

There is for Thoreau an aesthetic as well as a utilitarian result of the relation between the conditions of work and the product of work, and it leads him to deny aesthetic merit to the architectural monuments of antiquity. "As for the Pyramids, there is nothing to wonder at in them so much as the fact that so many men could be found degraded enough to spend their lives constructing a tomb for some ambitious booby, whom it would have been wiser and manlier to have drowned in the Nile and then given his body to the dogs" (*NA*, 1567). So the pyramids are impressive chiefly as a memorial to the degradation of Egyptian labor. Revolutionary regicide would have been a better reason for living than pyramid-building from the standpoint of the interests of the oppressed and from Thoreau's standpoint as well. So offended is Thoreau by the social meaning of the splendors of Egypt that he deflates them by likening them to American architectural statements of affluence and dominance. "As for the religion and love of art of the builders, it is much the same all the world over, whether the building be an Egyptian temple or a United States bank. It costs more than it comes to" (*NA*, 1567). And that cost is chiefly levied on the flesh and spirit of the oppressed.

This is architectural criticism as social criticism. The human costs of grandiose structures are likely to outweigh whatever aesthetic achievements they embody. And what they signify in the lives of the workers who made them is ever the first thing to catch Thoreau's attention.

> The myriads who built the Pyramids to be the tombs of the Pharaohs were fed on garlic, and it may be were not decently buried themselves. The mason who finishes the cornice of the palace returns at night perchance to a hut not so good as a wigwam. It is a mistake to suppose that, in a country where the usual advantages of civilization exist, the condition of a very large body of the inhabitants may not be as degraded as that of savages. . . . To know this I should not need to look farther than to the shanties which everywhere border our railroads, that last improvement in civilization. . . . It is certainly fair to look at that class by whose labor the works which distinguish this generation are accomplished. (*NA*, 1552)

The fall from the wigwam to the shanty accompanies the progress of civilization from running to railroading.

Most work Thoreau had seen or heard or read about and some that he had engaged in himself seemed too large and too poor for the spiritual and physical health of those performing it. It would, he thought, improve the worker's health and well-being if the fraction of life devoted to making a living could be reduced without doing away with work altogether. How far that reduction might go would be limited by work's being a human need as well as a supplier of necessities. Thoreau's ostensibly stoical, ascetic experiments in doing without some culturally defined "necessities" as well as his study of the historically changing scope of human needs were efforts to discover a standard of living that would permit him, and not only him, to minimize working time and maximize leisure time without violating the principle that work is a human need. His experiments in providing himself with food, shelter, and fuel were efforts to discover ways of working that would allow him the freest development of his humanity.

When he was a student at Harvard, Thoreau thought about the amount of time any human being ought to spend at work, and in one of his college assignments he challenges the biblical division of the week between labor and leisure days. "The order of things should be somewhat reversed—the seventh should be man's day of toil, wherein to earn his living by the sweat of his brow, and the other six his sabbath of the affections and the soul."[1] Thoreau's readiness to maximize leisure by overturning the traditional ratio of work to leisure is reaffirmed by his claim in *Walden* that "for more than five years . . . I found that, by working about six weeks in a year, I could meet all the expenses of living. The whole of my winters, as well as most of my summers, I had free and clear for study" (*NA*, 1574). Thoreau, if we accept this claim, returned to Concord to practice work and leisure in an annual pattern in which his projected ratio of six times more leisure than work was overfulfilled in an ratio approaching nine to one. In both theory and practice of working time, Thoreau went beyond Orestes Brownson, the friend and mentor of his college years. A labor radical and transcendentalist who had been a founder of the Workingmen's party of New York in 1827, Brownson in 1838 criticized a strike for the twelve-hour day on the grounds that the strikers ought to be demanding the six-hour day. Beyond six hours, thought Brownson, all toil is spiritually and physically harmful.[2] The ideas about working time from Brownson and Thoreau appear relatively modest when compared with J. A. Etzler's idea of an entirely workless world. Thoreau wrestles with that idea and finally rejects it in an 1843 review of Etzler's *The Paradise within the Reach of all Men, without Labor by Powers of Nature and Machinery.*

A German-American utopian, Etzler in his book set out "to show the means of creating a paradise within ten years, where everything desirable for human life may be had by every man in superabundance, without labor, without pay; where the whole face of nature shall be changed into the most beautiful forms and man may live in the most magnificent palaces, and in all imaginable refinements of luxury, and in the most delightful gardens; where he may accomplish without labor, in one year, more than could hitherto be done in a thousand years" (*ME*, 57–58). Thoreau's review of Etzler's book is largely sympathetic. Devoted as he was to a program of self-culture, Thoreau nevertheless grants that the efforts of the individual and the social reformer may be complementary. "While one scours the heavens, the other sweeps the earth. One says he will reform himself, and then nature and circumstances will be right. . . . The other will reform nature and circumstances, and then man will be right" (*ME*, 58). Then Thoreau momentarily goes beyond the thought that the two ways of change are complementary and approaches the view that man makes himself as he changes the world, the view Marx expresses in "Theses on Feuerbach." As Thoreau phrases the thought, "Undoubtedly if we were to reform this outward life truly and thoroughly, we should find no duty of the inner omitted. It would be the employment of our whole nature; and what we should do thereafter would be as vain a question as to ask a bird what it will do when its nest is built and its brood reared." These two sentences imply no priority for internal change over external change, or vice versa. They say that if we change the world, we shall not find ourselves unchanged and that a thorough transformation of human nature and its environment will leave us with nothing to do in the world. Yet if Thoreau could be entirely happy with this reading, he would not be the philosophical idealist he usually is. So he adds, "But a moral reform must take place first, and then the necessity for the other will be superseded, and we shall sail and plow by its force alone" (*ME,* 74). The effect of *But* is to cancel the sympathetic concession Thoreau has made to Etzler, and, by extension, to all who suppose that the expansion by technology of the productive forces is necessary if human needs are to be met. Thoreau goes on to cite Hindu scripture in support of the priority of moral reform: " 'It is not the same to one whose foot is enclosed in a shoe, as if the whole surface of the earth were covered with leather?' " (*ME,* 74). Intended by Thoreau to clinch the argument for the priority of individual moral reform over the transformation of the objective world, this rhetorical question can as well illustrate the limitations of a subjective view of reality. If the well-shod observer is aware that most of his fellow human beings are barefoot, the observer will possibly recognize that the surface of the earth is strewn with many objects potentially painful to the unprotected feet of other mortals.

Further along in his review of Etzler's book, Thoreau speculates on the world historical sabbath, which would afflict humanity if and when all the necessary work of the world can be finished. Etzler had forecast the invention of more durable building materials and Thoreau elaborates on the forecast, imagining the consequences:

> But why may not the dwellings of men on this earth be built, once for all . . . ? Why may we not finish the outside world for posterity, and leave them leisure to attend to the inner? Surely all the gross necessities might be cared for in a few years. All might be built and baked and stored up, during this, the term-time of the world, against the

> vacant eternity, and the globe go provisioned and furnished, like our public vessels, for its voyage through space, as through some Pacific Ocean, while we would "tie up the rudder and sleep before the wind." (*ME,* 76)

Humanity would then be in the situation of a bird "when its nest is built and its brood reared" and Thoreau is not pleased with the prospect. The image of humanity asleep at the rudder dispels the charm of unlimited leisure to attend to inner concerns in an entirely workless world. Thoreau is a man wishing to wake his neighbors up.

So he rejects Etzler's forecast that "all labor shall be reduced to 'a short turn of some crank' and 'taking the finished article away' " and he asserts that no "really important work can be made easier by cooperation or machinery. Not one particle of labor now threatening any man can be routed without being performed" (*ME,* 69–70). This oracular utterance is unaccompanied by clarifying illustration. One must look elsewhere in Thoreau for hints as to what important work means to him or as to how the intimation that labor is inescapable should be understood. For the moment, it is enough for Thoreau to assert that when technological innovation brings about a "vast application of forces," work will not disappear: "most things will have to be accomplished still by the application called Industry." It pleases Thoreau that there will always be a need in the world for human labor, that "constant and accumulated force which stands behind every spade in every field" (*ME,* 70). Humanity will avoid the fate of the bird that no longer has anything to do after its brood has flown the next. In Thoreau's utopia, contemplation and action will ever remain interdependent, inseparable aspects of life.

In *Walden* the contemplative rises out of the active. As with Goethe's Faust, so it is with Thoreau: "In the beginning was the deed." The deed in *Walden* is a man's providing himself with the means of life: building a house, gardening, hunting, fishing, and casual labor. These activities provide the experience, which may be transmuted into art and wisdom when they are undertaken deliberately and not in a routine, thoughtless, driven, alienated style. To penetrate, comprehend, and describe these activities, to contemplate and interpret them, requires review of the human past, the study of how such tasks were performed in past generations. Economic history for Thoreau is part of the solution to the problem of getting a satisfactory living. Without attention to this subject, neither a good understanding of the past nor a highly conscious and deliberate life in the present is possible. Thoreau's approach to history finds expression in a critical essay on Thomas Carlyle written in 1846 when Thoreau was living at Walden. Thoreau complains that Carlyle's *French Revolution* is too exclusively concerned with political events. Daily life does go on during a revolution, and the reader of Carlyle should be reminded that "the French peasantry did something besides go without breeches, burn chateaus, get ready knotted cords, and embrace and throttle one another by turns." He wishes Carlyle had thought to include in his book chapters on " 'Work for the Month,' " " 'State of the Crops and Markets,' " " 'Meteorological Observations,' " and " 'Day Labor' " (*ME,* 88).

Carlyle's account of the French Revolution seems to Thoreau to reveal an impairment of vision caused by the unwholesomeness of London, where Carlyle lives: "the sorest place on the face of the earth, the very citadel of conservatism." The condition of England narrows the scope of Carlyle's work. A writer cannot see humanity and nature whole living in such a place. "Until a thousand nameless grievances are righted, there will be no repose for him in the lap of Nature, or the seclusion of science and literature" (*ME,* 97). A writer living in an unjust society must act to right grievances before hoping to enjoy the repose needed for contemplation or the detachment for study. It is a duty, as Thoreau suggests in "Resistance to Civil Government," falling on anyone benefiting from or otherwise implicated in the infliction of wrongs. "If I devote myself to other pursuits and contemplations than the struggle for justice, I must see, at least, that I do not pursue them sitting upon another man's shoulders. I must get off him first, that he may pursue his contemplations." So Carlyle's living in "the sorest place on the face of the earth" limits his observer's range; even if he wanted to, he couldn't see life whole from that situation.

Thoreau, in the grip of utopian optimism about the possibilities of American life, believed that the repose and seclusion denied to Carlyle in England were available to writes "here in New England, where there are potatoes enough, and every man can get his living peacefully and sportively as the birds and bees, and need think no more of that" (*ME,* 97). Getting a living "peacefully and sportively" in New England was, as he knew, an unrealized possibility for most. Soon before or after writing his essay on Carlyle, Thoreau notes in his *Journal* that "everywhere in shops and offices and fields" people "seem to be doing penance in a thousand curious, unheard-of ways."[3] In *Walden* he generalizes that "it is a mistake to suppose that, in a country where the usual evidences of civilization exist, the condition of a very large body of the inhabitants may not be as degraded as that of savages." (*NA,* 1552). Later yet the sharpening of the crisis over slavery would wring from Thoreau the admission that "the remembrance of my country spoils my walk."[4] Consciousness of the enormous wrong that must be righted, in other words, reduced or ended his freedom to contemplate nature and focus on the particularities of everyday life.

Thoreau's essay on Carlyle includes a comparison of Carlyle and Emerson. The two writers "complement each other"—Carlyle is a man of action and Emerson is a contemplative man, but neither singly nor in combination do they satisfy the requirements of the times. Why not? Because neither Carlyle nor Emerson speaks to the condition of the "man of the Age, come to be called workingman, . . . for the speaker is not yet in his condition" (*ME,* 97). The writer who would speak to and celebrate the self-possessed humanity of a new age must himself possess the powers of action and contemplation of a worker enjoying the good working conditions that only a just society can provide. It is possible that Thoreau saw Carlyle as the right man in the wrong society—wrong because it narrowed his view of life—and that he saw Emerson as the wrong man in the right society—the wrong man because he was too passive and contemplative to seize the possibilities the environment offered him. In any event, the writer Thoreau calls for will accept Carlyle's injunction that "we had best be doing something in good earnest henceforth and forever" and will make use of Carlyle's revision of "[t]he before impossible precept, *'Know thyself,'* into the partially possible one, *'Know what thou canst work at'* " (*ME,* 99). The result, Thoreau predicts, would be "poetry . . . the only life got, the only work done, the only pure product and free labor of man, performed only when he has put the world under his feet, and conquered the last of his foes" (*ME,* 97). *Walden* has some claim to being poetry of this order. To a great extent it is the product of the free labor of a man whose active and contemplative life, whose work and art are marvelously integrated.

Thoreau was keenly aware that American and English ways of

getting a living in an industrializing market economy motivated by profit and operated by the division of labor was doing dehumanizing things to that part of the human race caught up in the system. The spectacle of the entire working population "doing penance in a thousand remarkable ways," first noted in his *Journal,* is the first image of the inhabitants of Concord that Thoreau presents in *Walden.* His working neighbors remind him of Hindu fakirs engaged in rituals of self-torture with the exception that working for a living in Concord is not a form of conscious penance, but Hindu ascetic humiliation of the flesh is. Working in Concord not only puts him in mind of patient endurance of torture but also of heroic expenditures of energy: "The twelve labors of Hercules were trifling in comparison with those which my neighbors have undertaken; for those were only twelve and had an end; but I could never see that these men slew or captured any monster or finished any labor" (*NA,* 1532). It was rather his working neighbors, in the performance of their tedious labors, who were caught and eaten up by a monstrous system.

The system tortures and exhausts those working in all sectors of the economy, agriculture included. Thoreau had met "many a poor immortal soul . . . well nigh crushed and smothered under its load, creeping down the road of life, pushing before it a barn seventy-five feet by forty, its Augean stables never cleansed, and one hundred acres of land, tillage, mowing, pasture, and wood lot" (*NA,* 1533). Back to the land, then, is no remedy for the condition of the workers: "From the desperate city you go into the desperate country. . . . But it is characteristic of wisdom not to do desperate things" (*NA,* 1535). How and why does all this agony persist and what hope is there that something effective might be done about it? For Thoreau the problem is consciousness:

> Most men, even in this comparatively free country, through mere ignorance and mistake, are so occupied with the factitious cares and superfluously coarse labors of life that its finer fruits cannot be plucked by them. Their fingers, from excessive toil, are too clumsy and tremble too much for that. Actually, the laboring man has not leisure for a true integrity day by day; he cannot afford to maintain the manliest relations to men; his labor would be depreciated in the market. He has no time to be anything but a machine. How can he remember well his ignorance—which has growth requires—who has so often to use his knowledge? (*NA,* 1533)

Behind this analysis is an assumption common to all revolutionary propaganda and agitation: if only they can wake up—if knowledge can replace error in their minds—rational action can replace tradition in their lives and then the oppressed can free themselves. "[T]o wake my neighbors up" is one of the intentions Thoreau announces in the epigraph to *Walden.* Until they are awake to their condition, "excessive toil" robs them of the skill and nerve that must be exerted if life is to be fully lived. Until then they remain stunted and fragmented beings cringing under the whip of the market, their development arrested. Like most revolutionary propagandists, Thoreau does little to resolve the perplexity about how to hasten the awakening, the liberating leap in consciousness. He does, however, tell us three things about the struggle for emancipation from stultifying labor. First, it will be more the work of dissatisfied individuals than it will be a cooperative struggle. These are the "poor students" whom he identifies as his primary audience, a group whose curiosity about the world and its possibilities is not distorted by their possessing a material stake in things as they are. Second, it will require the expansion of leisure time through the reduction, but not the elimination, of the working day and year. Third, it will require the acquisition of a playful, studious style of work.

Acquiring a new style of work, getting rid of stultifying labor, begins for Thoreau with the reduction, but not the elimination, of the division of labor. He treats in this connection two aspects of the division of labor, the split between mental and manual labor and the breaking up of a work process into components performed by different workers. The division of labor, according to Thoreau, is "a principle which should never be followed but with circumspection" (*NA,* 1562). Followed unconditionally, it makes for workers unfit for leisure and students unfit for study.

To illustrate how mental and manual labor might be combined, Thoreau suggests that the students of a new college should take a hand in erecting its buildings. He does not mean that "the students should go to work with their hands instead of their heads" but "that they should not *play* life or *study* it merely, while the community supports them in this expensive game." Without the combination of manual work and study, students suffer intellectually and morally. "The student who secures his coveted leisure and retirement by systematically shirking any labor necessary to man obtains but an ignoble and unprofitable leisure, defrauding himself of the experience which alone can make leisure fruitful" (*NA*, 1562–63). Thoreau takes for granted that the community ought to support higher education but not in a style that intensifies the division of labor. His scheme for the erection of college buildings requires a collaborative effort involving a circumspect division of labor. "To act collectively is according to the spirit of our institutions," he writes when advocating a system of adult education by which "New England can hire all the wise men in the world to come and teach her" (*NA*, 1600). This example, too, leaves room for the survival of the division between mental and manual labor, for the community apparently will hire the wise men without requiring them to earn their keep by manual labor. For himself, Thoreau eschewed this kind of specialization. For him, the norm of unalienated humanity is the worker whose mind and muscle are equally taxed and who cooperates with the other workers without enslaving them or being enslaved by them.

Thoreau distinguishes two senses of the term *cooperation;* one is common and low, the other rare and high: "The only cooperation which is commonly possible is exceedingly partial and superficial; and what little true cooperation there is, is as if it were not, being a harmony inaudible to men" (*NA*, 1576). The worker experiencing cooperation in its "commonly possible" form lives, "like the rest of the world whatever company he is joined to." He will, that is, always experience the hierarchy of commanders and subordinates that inheres in the historical forms of social labor. "Abandon autonomy, all ye who enter here,"[5] the inscription proposed by Engels as appropriate for factory gates, would have seemed to Thoreau appropriate for all until now devised ways of organizing social labor.

In contrast to the commonly possible form of cooperation are the rare instances of "true cooperation," in which sovereign individuals come together in an association so free of constraints as to form "a harmony inaudible to men." It is probably invisible and indescribable as well, being located in that unrealized kingdom of freedom alluded to in the *Communist Manifesto,* in which "the free development of each is the condition of the free development of all."[6] Thoreau's definition of cooperation, then, includes the antitheses slavery and freedom, subordination and equality. His true cooperation, cooperation in its highest sense, will prevail only among emancipated workers; among others, only the commonly possible kind of cooperation will exist. Hence, getting our living together in freedom requires the prior success of our separate efforts at self-culture. To adapt the phrase from the *Manifesto,* the existence of a free society is conditional on "the free development" of each member of it. Individual free development, in turn, requires healing the split between mental and manual labor.

It also requires an attack on the aspect of the division of labor that breaks up a work process into components performed by different workers. Lessened dependence on the division of labor in this sense, in Thoreau's expectation, will stimulate creativity.

> Who knows but if men constructed their own dwellings with their own hands, and provided food for themselves and families simply and honestly enough, the poetic faculty would be universally developed, as birds universally sing when they are so engaged. But alas! we do like cowbirds and cuckoos, which lay their eggs in nests which other birds have built, and cheer no traveller with their chattering and unmusical notes. Shall we forever resign the pleasure of construction to the carpenter? What does architecture amount to in the experience of the mass of men?" (*NA,* 1559)

A major theme of *Walden* is a man's repossession of the "pleasure of construction" of which he has been dispossessed through the unchecked extension of the division of labor. Repossess that pleasure, Thoreau suggests, and the work process and the material worked on may become a mine of images and a supplier of rhythms uniting the physical and mental worlds so that nature may be represented as the symbol of the spirit. Maintaining himself by the labor of his hands mostly, Thoreau demonstrated in *Walden* that he could fashion a work of art more musical than the chattering of the alienated, fragmented victims of the division of labor. An examination of the literary uses he made of his house-building experience supports the conclusion that this is one of the things he set out to do in the writing of *Walden.*

House-building, as described in *Walden,* begins with the collecting of building materials. Thoreau first fells timber for his house frame. Then he buys the shanty of an Irish railroad worker, knocks it apart and carts the usable boards to his building site. In this proceeding, Thoreau is an Emersonian American scholar: his first resource is nature as newly felled trees; only after going to nature does he go to the past as the second-hand materials of the shanty. These, too, he uses in the prescribed Emersonian manner: he takes the old structure apart, selects what he needs and rejects what he does not, then combines the materials of the past with the materials cut freshly from nature, incorporating them into a new structure of his designing. Another debt Thoreau owed Emerson is suppressed in *Walden*. Thoreau there describes himself as a squatter on his building site, and the term denotes a user of land who does not ask permission for using it. But the land Thoreau built on was Emerson's and his building on it was part of a deal between the two men. In exchange for permission to live in Emerson's woods, Thoreau undertook to clear a field for gardening. This is one of the few instances in *Walden* in which the complaint that Thoreau exaggerates his independence of benefactors appears well grounded. Still, he was in this instance a party to a deal and not a recipient of charity. And in his narration he is bent on celebrating the pioneer on the frontier between nature and civilization, who makes circumspect use of the division of labor in getting his living. Sometimes historical detail gets in the way of the truth that inheres in myth.

Thoreau goes about the construction of his house deliberately. Finding out and reflecting on what others before him have done for shelter, he weighs the value and meaning of what he is going to do beforehand, thinks about the significance of each step in the process while he is doing it, and reflects further about his performance after it is completed. At least that is the impression of his work habits conveyed in *Walden*, for in writing it, he drew on his experience and his reading and writing for several years before and after the building of his house as well as on what he learned and wrote while building and living in it. Although it may not be possible to distinguish sharply his anticipatory and reflective thoughts about housebuilding from those striking him while engaged in carpentering and bricklaying, the relationship between his thoughts and actions falls into a pattern: thought is tested and elaborated through action. It is a Hegelian triadic progression of thought passing into practice and giving rise to practice-enriched thought. Thoreau at work on his house is the epitome of working humanity fulfilling a necessary function in a free and rational manner. Engaging his mind as fully as possible in the process, he works with the greatest deliberation and a minimum of mindless spontaneity. He illustrates the distinction made by Marx between the hive-making bee and the architect who "raises his structure in imagination before raising it in reality."[7]

Thoreau's first work on his house, felling timber close to his house site with a borrowed ax, is reported in *Walden* in a passage full of hints about his attitude toward work. He sharpens the borrowed ax not merely as a favor to its owner, but also because ease and efficiency in working are values that he cares about. He has pleasant working conditions: "a pleasant hillside" and "pleasant spring days in which the winter of man's discontent is thawing as well as the earth." The simple manual labor of felling trees is thawing Thoreau's discontent with civilization as well, while snow flurries changing to rain signal the transition from winter to spring. His working with borrowed tools (it is not only the ax that he borrows) emphasizes his status as a civilized man transforming natural materials. We all work with what has been lent or given us to use. Still, Thoreau can be at one with nature in these circumstances. He identifies with a snake in the pond when he soaks and swells a new ax handle there. The snake has taken refuge in the pond and lies there "perhaps because he had not yet fairly come out of the torpid state" (*NA*, 1556). Cutting and hewing studs, rafters, and floor timbers, Thoreau does not have "many communicable or scholar-like thoughts." Yet he can chant to the rhythm of the ax. It is a poem about practical and theoretical knowledge and about how, beyond intellectual and sensual apprehension, a more certain knowledge comes to us directly out of nature.

> Men say they know many things;
> But lo! they have taken wings— The arts and sciences,
> And a thousand appliances;
> The wind that blows
> Is all that anybody knows. (*NA*, 1557)

Thoreau's next step, after preparing his timbers, is to buy and cart away the James Collins shanty. As a source of boards and as an illustration of Thoreau's use of materials, the Collins shanty has a threefold significance. First, Thoreau's use of it is an example of his circumspect reliance on the division of labor. In his circumstances and despite his admiration for log cabins, it is simpler for him to use boards from the Collins shanty than to hew them by hand. Without them and without dependence on the sawmill that produced them,

Thoreau could not have had his house finished soon enough to spend the winter of 1845–46 at Walden Pond. Second, his use of the Collins shanty demonstrates a thrifty resort to secondhand materials, which, as it turns out, is no obstacle to designing and building a structure serving the needs of the person living in it. Third, use of the Collins shanty begins Thoreau's demonstration of how conventional, secondhand materials may be put to a better use than they have been; those materials become the unimproved means to an improved end. Using the boards from the "dark, . . . dank, clammy, and aguish" (*NA,* 1558). Collins shanty, represented in ***Walden*** as clearly unfit for a nuclear family sharing it with its chickens and cat, Thoreau builds "a tight shingled and plastered house, ten feet wide by fifteen long and eight-feet posts, with a garret and a closet, a large window on each side, two trap doors, one door at the end, and a brick fireplace opposite." The fireplace bricks and the windows are also secondhand; the shingles are "refuse" from a sliced log (*NA,* 1561).

Thoreau's use of the materials of the Collins shanty has three limiting conditions. Some of the material is rotten: there is "here a board and there a board which will not bear removal." Second, Thoreau must cart away what he can use of the shanty quickly before Collins's creditors appear to put in their "indistinct and wholly unjust claims on the score of ground rent and fuel." (If the shanty of this Irish railroad worker was close to the train tracks, the claimants might have included the Fitchburg Railroad, Collins's employer, in which case Thoreau's transaction with Collins was a conspiracy enabling a worker to get back from his employer a little of the profit made from the worker's labor.) Third, Thoreau has to contend with the danger that an unemployed Irish worker watching him demolish the shanty will filch some useful stuff before Thoreau can move it all to his building site. "Neighbor Seeley, . . . in the intervals of the carting, transferred the still tolerable, straight, and drivable nails, staples, and spikes to his pocket, and then stood when I came back to pass the time of day," having nothing better to do, "there being a dearth of work, as he said." Thoreau knows where these items disappeared to because another Irish bystander "treacherously" snitches on Seeley (*NA,* 1558).

Arriving at his building site by the pond, Thoreau spreads his sound boards "on the grass there to bleach and warp back in the sun." Thus, nature collaborates with the worker, rectifying and cleansing moldy encrustation from the materials he has acquired from Collins, making them fit for use. The symbolism of this simple work becomes apparent. Thoreau's taking possession of the shanty is a model of how free use is made of inherited culture. In quest of the kingdom of freedom, humankind assimilates materials passed on from the past by disassembling (analyzing) those materials, rejecting the rotten, purifying the sound, and combining what is to be used with new materials taken directly from nature. In this way, inherited materials can be used in new structures according to the needs of variegated, developing human nature. His taking possession of the Collins shanty is a "seemingly insignificant event" that Thoreau nevertheless identifies "with the removal of the gods of Troy" (*NA*, 1558). It is an event that links the destruction of one human habitation with the erection of another. The ruin of Troy and the founding of Rome are reenacted in the metamorphosis of the Collins shanty into the Thoreau cabin. Preserving the usable from the past in constructing the present is an epic endeavor, a labor for a hero. Setting out for Italy at the destruction of Troy by the Greeks, Aeneas had salvaged and carted away the city's gods. Thoreau is his own Greek demolition crew and his own Aeneas, but also his own Romulus, nurtured in the wilds and imbued with the vigor to renovate culture and found a new city. If he did not renew the world in fact but only in imagination, that failing only identifies him more closely with the heroes of mythology.

The shaping of culture is simultaneously a rising out of nature and a burrowing into it. After collecting his building materials, Thoreau's next step in house building is to dig a cellar. He digs "where a woodchuck had formerly dug his burrow." This digging, then, is an elaboration on, an augmentation of, the animal's efforts. It is work that follows nature in a strict sense of the phrase. The cellar digging is "but two hours work." Here is a boast that celebrates both animal vigor and skill. Displacing 252 cubic feet of dirt in two hours, an area six feet square to a depth of seven feet, is possible of accomplishment by a strong man handy with a shovel if he works in sandy soil. It certainly is not an example of Thoreau taking his time and taking things easy. Instead, it illustrates that Thoreau, like most workers, approaches some tasks with the thought that they are best finished quickly in a great surge of effort. Digging holes in the ground is not an inspiring job, but Thoreau reports that he "took particular pleasure in this breaking of ground, for in almost all latitudes men dig in the earth for an equable temperature" (*NA*, 1558). Notice that little pleasure in this work derives from skilled, efficient use of muscle power and none at all from any possible novelty of the experience (assuming this to be the first cellar Thoreau ever dug); on the contrary, the pleasure chiefly derives from the universality of a job, performed by workers expressing their need to master the weather and the seasons. Digging the cellar is humanizing labor for Thoreau in that it heightens the worker's sense of membership in the human species. To dig a hole in the ground is to do what human beings necessarily and constantly do; it is to assert one's species identity. At the same time, it reminds Thoreau of the unbreakable link between human culture and nature as represented by the woodchuck and his burrow. "Under the most splendid house in the city is still to be found the cellar where they store roots as of old, and long after the superstructure has disappeared posterity remarks its dent in the earth. The house is still but a sort of porch at the entrance of a burrow" (*NA*, 1559).

Thoreau frames his house the easiest way: he builds the walls flat on the ground and then raises them upright. Raising walls is hard for one worker to accomplish unassisted, but Thoreau suggests he could have done it by himself if he had cared to. It is "rather to improve so good an occasion for neighborliness than from any necessity" that he calls on friends to help set up his frame. In charming compliment to Emerson and Alcott, the younger W. E. Channing and George and William Curtis, he writes, "No man was ever more honored in the character of his raisers than I. They are destined, I trust, to assist at the raising of loftier structures one day" (*NA*, 1559). Given the relative unhandiness of these friends, it may be that their contribution to Thoreau's raising was more ceremonial than practical. However, there can be no question that they were Thoreau's intellectual raisers and fully deserve the compliment.

Thoreau moved into an unfinished house on July 4, 1845, "as soon as it was boarded and roofed, for the boards were carefully feather-edged and lapped, so that it was perfectly impervious to rain." Though unfinished as a year-round habitation, it was "finished" as a shelter against July weather. Thoreau will not call himself an inhabitant of the house until a later stage in its construction when it is proof against cold as well as rain. Further work on the house proceeds in synchronization with the passing of the seasons toward winter. Everything is done in the nick of time. Thus the requirement for comfort in July is simply a house "perfectly impervious to the rain." It cannot be warmed at this stage, because only the foundation of the chimney has been laid and there are drafty chinks between the boards of the walls; there is no need as yet that it should be capable of being warmed. Building the chimney came later, "after my hoeing in the fall, before a fire became necessary for warmth." He cooked "meanwhile out of doors on the ground" (*NA,* 1561, 1584). In these proceedings he follows a rational order of priorities. The securing of his food and cash crop from the bean field must be attended to before the work on the house can continue. Completion of the chimney exemplifies his nick-of-time relationship to the weather. He finishes it before the onset of cold weather and then supplements this defense against cold with an application of plaster to his chinky wall boards. In the second winter, he will improve the efficiency of his heating system by substituting a wood stove for the open fire.

In the year he built his house, Thoreau's working in harmony with the cycle of the seasons may also be regarded as subordination to nature, for the approach of winter limits the time he can spend making his house fit for year-round living. Nature thus dictates the pace of his work, and the simultaneous or alternating demands of his agriculture and of his carpentering and masonry force him to depart from the ideal condition of man working and thinking. "In those days, when my hands were much employed, I read but little," he confesses. Was this a price exacted for a too thorough forswearing of the division of labor? Was a journey to the frontier of economic independence compatible with scholarship and literary creativity? If such questions were in his mind, he does not disclose that they were. Instead, he boasts that in the circumstances of exhausting manual labor, "the least scrap of paper which lay on the ground, my holder, or tablecloth, afforded me as much entertainment, in fact answered the same purpose as the Iliad" (*NA,* 1559). Yet this claim is put forward by a man drained by toil of the energy required to read anything more demanding than a newspaper. In making it, he records his variant of the experience of workers who come off the job and sit in front of the television, able to absorb only its undemanding messages. Because true leisure, in Thoreau's view, comes only as a diversion from dignified work, working heroically invests every entertainment with heroism, enriching even the most trivial object of contemplation. If few of us now respond to the mass media creatively, perhaps it is because few working in the contemporary economy believe their labors are heroic.

In an acceptance of conditions on and off the job, we are not unlike those Concord neighbors of Thoreau's, going through their daily punishments "in shops, and offices, and fields" with seemingly endless patience, under Thoreau's astonished eyes. And in our potentialities we are not unlike them either. Through his cabin window Thoreau regularly observed the maintenance crew of the railroad that ran along the shore of Walden Pond opposite his building site. Watching them, he thought of the human cost of the railroad, seeing in the maintenance crew a symbol of the state and, in the millions of wooden ties under the rails, a symbol of a prostrate working class that nevertheless retains its ability to take back its alienated humanity in a revolutionary rising:

> We do not ride on the railroad; it rides upon us. Did you ever think what those sleepers are that underlie the railroad? Each one is a man, an Irish man or a Yankee man. The rails are laid on them, and they are covered with sand, and the cars run smoothly over them. They are sound sleepers, I assure you. And every few years a new lot is laid down and run over; so that if some have the pleasure of riding on a rail, others have the misfortune to be ridden upon. . . . I am glad to know that it takes a gang of men for every five miles to keep the sleepers down and level in their beds, for this is a sign that they may sometime get up again. (*NA*, 1589)

Having made a house fit for all seasons, Thoreau discovered along the way, and later demonstrated, that his unalienated work was productive of much more than a simple shelter. That work provided him with a vantage point from which to better realize his own humanity, to get a good view of the labors and contemplations of others, and to turn his experience and study into great art.

2.

The Floating Factory Sinks

LIKE A WESTERN high-noon confrontation, Captain Ahab's final encounter with the White Whale belongs in the American treasury of rugged individualist hero fables. In those American duels the seconds called for in the European dueling code are customarily dispensed with. That is how the matter stands in the mind of Ahab: single combat—Ahab versus Moby-Dick. Ahab's last words to Ishmael and the "tiger-yellow barbarians" who make up the boat crew who row him toward the whale are "Ye are not other men, but my arms and legs: and so obey me" (chapter 135).[1]

But the conflict is not seen this way by Ishmael, the narrator in *Moby-Dick*. Ishmael keeps in mind that the disastrous confrontation with the whale requires the presence and submissive cooperation of the thirty mariners in the *Pequod*'s crew. Ishmael occasionally shifts the reader's attention from the monomaniac captain's pursuit of a single whale. He then views the action aboard the *Pequod* from the powerless depths of the forecastle rather than from the commanding heights of the quarterdeck.

With this shift in point of view the problem of work and what it does to workers assumes importance in *Moby-Dick*. The novel then appears to be partly about sailors ridden by the routine of their craft, whose souls are subject to dollars, who are manipulated like the rope of a ship, and who, as sometimes enthusiastic, sometimes sullen or apathetic tools of their commander's vengeance, cooperate in their own destruction. Ishmael assumes the obligation to explain how this fatal cooperation comes about. It is an insider's explanation, for Ishmael shares in all the attitudes expressed by other members of the crew toward their commander and his cruise. If Ishmael stands apart from his shipmates, it is principally because he has more skill or luck at avoiding being sweated by speedup and fragmented by the division of labor than his shipmates. His upper-class origins also makes him less accustomed to the despotism inflicted on ordinary seamen than are most of them. Ishmael is an intellectual in an unskilled job, who thinks about what he is working at and thinks about his fellow workers as well as about Ahab and Ahab's heroic quest.

Among many other things *Moby-Dick* is a novel about an industrializing country. It epitomizes economic development in its representation of the history and lore of one major industry. Like all profound social criticism it is prophetic as well as descriptive. To many readers the *Pequod,* that "cannibal of a craft, tricked out in the chased bones of her enemies" (16), is perhaps too gothic, too romantically wonderful, to be thought of as a factory. But in the era before kerosene and gas lamps and the incandescent tungsten filament, the business of supplying sperm oil for lighting the country was comparable for the economy to what electric companies do now. Abstract the *Pequod*'s function momentarily from the economic particulars of the 1840s and embody it in its present equivalent, and the economic significance of the ship might be more readily seen. A modern parallel to the *Pequod* would be an antiquated but still functional power plant. It is a dangerous place to work. It is run by a cunning, duplicitous manager who has lost interest in the usual capitalist purpose of such a plant. Though he is one of them, this manager no longer cares about marketing power to make a profit for the owners. Maimed in his work and brooding on his maiming, the manager runs the plant on dead reckoning or diabolical inspiration more than he does by aid of rational science and technology. Vengeance on what he perceives to be the cause of his misery replaces supplying the market and enriching the owners as motive for doing business. In pursuit of vengeance the manager is reckless with the lives of the workers. Combining mystification with material incentives, he keeps the work force obedient to his commands. Finally, in consequence of his insane abuse of his authority, the power plant blows up. Manager and workers perish, except one worker who lives to report the disaster. So might go a modern variant of the fable of the *Pequod.* But whether in such a variant or in its original version, the

Pequod's fable is deeply concerned with the American work experience. *Moby-Dick* is prophetic though not necessarily predictive. It speaks of possible, not inevitable, developments from the American work experience. Though very American, the *Pequod* is not the only American ship, as Ishmael is careful to tell us, nor is hers the only possible American cruise.

In *Moby-Dick* Ishmael presents several possible courses open to the expanding industrial capitalism within which he lives and works. He does this by telling the stories of other American whale ships the *Pequod* encounters at sea. Of these the first is the homeward-bound *Goney,* or *Albatross.* What is striking about the *Goney* is her weather-beaten appearance, evidence of her "nearly four years of cruising." She "was bleached like the skeleton of a stranded walrus. All down her sides, this spectral appearance was traced with long channels of reddened rust, while all her spars and her rigging were like thick branches of trees furred over with hoar-frost" (52). Ishmael is one of the three men aloft on the *Pequod*'s mastheads when she and the *Goney* pass each other. To him the *Goney*'s "long-bearded look-outs . . . seemed clad in the skins of beasts." At the closest approach of the two vessels "we six men in the air came so nigh to one another that we might almost have leaped from the mastheads of one ship to those of the other; yet, those forlorn-looking fishermen, mildly eyeing us as they passed, said not one word to our own look-outs." Meanwhile, down below there is incomplete communication between the two quarterdecks. Ahab can be heard by the captain of the *Goney* but that captain loses his speaking trumpet overboard and cannot make his voice carry to the *Pequod* (52). For the *Goney*'s lookouts there is either no desire for communication or no ability for it; for her captain only the ability is lacking. With respect to the *Goney*'s lookouts—their beards, their clothes, their silence—the suggestion is that their long, isolating work experience has thrust them back into the earliest state of nature that is the infancy, the nonverbal epoch, of human prehistory. In this suggestion there is no hint of sentimental rhapsodizing over the primitivizing results of oppressive labor. Appropriately the captain is less victim of alienation than his crew; his powers of speech are less impaired than theirs.

Another ship crossing the *Pequod*'s path and homeward bound is the *Bachelor.* Embodying the American dream of success, she presents an image of joyous idleness. Every possible space aboard the *Bachelor* is crammed with full barrels of sperm oil. She has "met with surprising success; all the more wonderful, for that while cruising in the same seas numerous other vessels had gone entire months without securing a single fish." The *Bachelor* is no longer a factory. From the forecastle of this lucky ship comes "the barbarian sound of enormous drums." These are the ship's try-pots, now converted into tympani. The rest of the tryworks, which cannot be made to serve the purposes of celebration, are chucked overboard. Of the part of the *Bachelor's* crew that is noisily taking the tryworks apart, Ishmael remarks, "You would have almost thought they were pulling down the cursed Bastille, such wild cries they raised, as the now useless brick and mortar were being hurled into the sea." Meanwhile, three Long Island black seamen fiddle up a "hillarious jig" and the mates and harpooneers dance with "olive-hued girls who had eloped with them from the Polynesian Isles." All this is simultaneously a kind of Luddite parody of the insurrectional beginning of the French Revolution and an enactment of the American dream in which, after making a killing, men retire to a paradise of sensual idleness, more jazzy than lazy, an orgiastic Gatsby party. The captain of the *Bachelor* has heard of the White Whale but does not believe in him and would likely not believe in the existence of the *Pequod* herself, if told how and why she is managed by Ahab (115).

The *Jeroboam* presents another variant of American destiny. She bears the name of a king of Israel who, like Ahab, is a wicked rebel against God. Aboard the *Jeroboam* as aboard the *Pequod* the Jeffersonian motto might be appropriate: resistance to tyrants is obedience to God. Yet there are significant differences in the situations aboard the two ships. When the *Pequod* encounters the *Jeroboam* the authority of her profit-oriented captain has been overthrown by a Neskyeuna Shaker seaman who calls himself Gabriel. This seaman assumes the archangelic function by announcing that the White Whale is the incarnation of God, that to hunt him is therefore impious, and that any who do are doomed to destruction. In important ways Gabriel's role and views are a mirror image of Ahab's. To infiltrate a ship cruising for profit, Gabriel, like Ahab, must pass himself off as a man of common sense "with that cunning peculiar to craziness." Once safely at sea, and having revealed his true calling after it is too late for the ship's owners to do anything about it,

Gabriel "was not of much practical use in the ship, especially as he refused to work except when he pleased." The *Jeroboam*'s captain tries to get rid of Gabriel but is frustrated when the crew en masse "went to the captain and told him that if Gabriel was sent from the ship, not a man of them would remain." The *Jeroboam* represents an America in the grip of an apocalyptic religious revival. Under Gabriel's sway she veers away from profit-taking as the locus of value but on a course opposite to the one steered by the *Pequod* under Ahab. For Ahab and his followers killing the White Whale is an honorable, glorious, saving action; for Gabriel and his followers it is damnable. Gabriel also distances the *Jeroboam* from the common American dream typified by the *Bachelor:* for the *Bachelor* withdrawal from the profitable hunt is the reward for making a killing; for the *Jeroboam* withdrawal is the alternative to making a killing. Joyous satiety prevails aboard the *Bachelor;* apocalyptic horror prevails among the crew of the *Jeroboam.* Among revolts against a captain's authority meditated or tried aboard American whale ships described by Ishmael, the revolt aboard the *Jeroboam* is the only one that is entirely successful (71). With the *Jeroboam,* as with the *Pequod,* the course sailed by the ship is determined by the delusions of a cunning fanatic, by his vision of the supernatural whale—for Gabriel, reverent; for Ahab, raging.

Next to the *Pequod,* the variant of American destiny Ishmael elaborates most fully is that represented by the ship *Town-Ho.* Hers is a businesslike name, "town-ho" being an "ancient whale-cry upon first sighting a whale from the mast-head." When she meets the *Pequod,* the *Town-Ho* is homeward bound toward Nantucket "manned almost wholly by Polynesians." This is not the same crew she started her cruise with. There has been a mutiny aboard the *Town-Ho* and Ishmael provides a detailed analysis of it (54).

The Polynesian majority of the *Town-Ho*'s crew do not know the history of the mutiny. "It was the private property of three confederate white seamen of that ship, one of whom, it seems, communicated it to Tashtego," the *Pequod*'s American Indian harpooneer. Ishmael's information about the mutiny comes from Tashtego and, later, from Steelkilt, the leader of the mutiny. When the two ships meet, the officers of the *Town-Ho* and the *Pequod* exchange news and pleasantries but the story of the mutiny "never reached the ears of Ahab or his mates." Ishmael perhaps implies that those in authority are inclined to keep quiet about revolts when possible. In contrast to the encounter between the *Pequod* and the *Goney,* more communication transpires between the crews of the *Pequod,* and the *Town-Ho* than between their officers. Does the tradition of revolt help rescue its bearers from speechlessness?

The origin of the *Town-Ho* mutiny, in Ishmael's analysis, is that the ship is run on the principle of business as usual under circumstances that unnecessarily endanger the lives of all on board. The ship has sprung a leak.

> But the captain, having some unusual reason for believing that rare good luck awaited him . . . the ship still continued her cruisings, the mariners working at the pumps at wide and easy intervals; but no good luck came; more days went by, and not only was the leak undiscovered, but it sensibly increased. So much so, that now taking some alarm, the captain, making all sail, stood away for the nearest harbor among the islands, there to have his hull hove out and repaired.

Though the captain has risked drowning the crew in his unsafe ship for the sake of maximizing profits, that policy by itself is not enough to provoke a mutiny. To the anxiety, exhaustion, and resentment of the men who must daily work the pumps for longer and longer stretches, some other element must be added before a social explosion is produced. In this instance it is the personal antagonism between the first mate Radney, who is a part owner of the ship, and Steelkilt, a harpooneer. In one of Ishmael's images of contrast Steelkilt suggests a "viceroy's snorting charger" and Radney is "ugly as a mule; yet as hardy, as stubborn, as malicious." Ishmael generalizes the clash between these two as an instance of the tendency of a supervisor to persecute a skilled worker who thinks too well of himself.

> [I]t is not seldom the case in this conventional world of ours—watery or otherwise; that when a person placed in command over his fellow-men finds one of them to be very significantly his superior in general pride of manhood, straightway against that man he conceives an unconquerable dislike and bitterness; and if he has a chance he will pull down and pulverize that subaltern's tower, and make a little heap of dust of it.

Steelkilt feels Radney's animosity and his response is to ridicule the mate. While working at the pump Steelkilt talks to his fellow workers about Radney, knowing the mate is near and will overhear:

> [I]t's a lively leak this. . . . The fact is, boys, that . . . a gang of ship-carpenters, saw-fish, and file-fish, and what not . . . are hard at work cutting and slashing at the bottom; making improvements, I suppose. If old Rad were here now, I'd tell him to jump overboard and scatter 'em. They're playing the devil with his estate, I can tell him. But he's a simple old soul,—Rad, and a beauty too. Boys, they say the rest of his property is invested in looking-glasses.

This irreverence provokes Radney to pull his rank. Finishing his turn at the pump, the exhausted Steelkilt "went forward, and sat himself down on the windlass, his face fiery red, his eyes bloodshot, and wiping profuse sweat from his brow." At that moment, "intolerably striding along the deck, the mate commanded him to get a broom and sweep down the planks, and also a shovel" to clean away the dung of a pig allowed to run loose on deck. The mate's command is a provocation on two counts. First, as a harpooneer Steelkilt is a skilled worker to whom the command is an affront to his caste dignity. "[I]n all vessels this broom business is the prescriptive province of the boys, if boys there be aboard." Second, none of the *Town-Ho*'s boys are tired out from working the pumps. "[I]t was the stronger men in the Town-Ho that had been divided into gangs, taking turns at the pumps; and being the most athletic seaman of them all, Steelkilt had been regularly assigned captain of one of the gangs; consequently he should have been freed from any trivial business not connected with truly nautical duties, such being the case with his comrades." It is understood by Steelkilt and his shipmates that "the order about the shovel was almost plainly meant to sting and insult Steelkilt, as though Radney had spat in his face."

Unfortunately for Radney and the rest of the officers, Steelkilt, who had been a rowdy boatman along the Erie Canal before shipping aboard the *Town-Ho,* is a natural workers' leader. Admired by the crew, he inspires resistance to degrading authority. His own authority has a fraternal quality and does not rest on his being "a nameless terror" (71) to the crew, as with the *Jeroboam*'s Gabriel. It is also true that his authority over the *Town-Ho*'s crew is not as complete as Gabriel's authority over the *Jeroboam*'s. The latter's crew back Gabriel to a man, but only a third of the *Town-Ho*'s crew back Steelkilt when, inevitably, he refuses to obey the mate's insulting order, breaks Radney's jaw, violently resists arrest, and, with nine of his followers, seizes control of the forecastle deck, "where, hastily slewing about three of four large casks in a line with the windlass, these sea-Parisians entrenched themselves behind the barricades." The revolt Steelkilt leads, like most workers' uprisings in history, is purely defensive. The mutineers never overpower the officers, never take over the quarterdeck. They are not armed with guns. The captain would shoot Steelkilt but for fear that his "death would be the signal for a murderous mutiny on the part of all hands." The demand of the mutineers is modest: they will submit to the restoration of order and discipline in return for amnesty. Mounting the barricade, Steelkilt parleys with the captain as spokesman for the part of the crew that has the legal right to leave the ship at the first port of call: "[S]ir, we can claim our discharges as soon as the anchor is down; so we don't want a row; it's not in our interest; we want to be peaceable; we are ready to work, but we won't be flogged."

At this stage, two-thirds of the crew are neutral spectators to the struggle between mutineers and officers. When Steelkilt's offer is rejected, the mutineers, ever on the defensive, retreat into the forecastle hold. Penned in there, the forecastle hatch locked shut, the solidarity of the mutineers gradually dissolves. Four of the ten surrender, then another three; finally—in an act evocative of the Hebrew surrender of Samson to the Philistines at Lehi—two of the last three tie up Steelkilt and turn him over to the captain in the unfounded hope that their treachery will save them from punishment.

The revolt aboard the *Town-Ho* and its suppression illuminate contrasting conditions aboard the *Pequod* and also the views of Ishmael (and probably of Melville) about the prospect for a proletarian revolution in capitalist America. As in the *Town-Ho,* in the *Pequod* there are instances of provocative and demeaning orders being issued; however, there are no instances of such orders being refused. An example is Second Mate Stubb's directions to Fleece on how to prepare a whale steak for Stubb's supper, followed by his command that the old black cook lean over the ship's side and preach a pacifying sermon on brotherhood to the sharks (64). The reception of those commands shows the recipient to be an old and broken man, incapable of defiance. But young or old, men on board the *Pequod* are under control and do what they are told. There is no one aboard the *Pequod* with a temperament comparable to Steelkilt's, though there had been at the outset of the voyage: the heroic and beloved

Bulkington, the man from the Blue Ridge of Virginia and leader of the *Pequod*'s crew. Melville drowns him early in the voyage (23). After the providential elimination of Bulkington there is no one in the doomed *Pequod* to be catalyst and leader of opposition to Ahab. This says that there is more likelihood of revolt in a business-as-usual America like that represented by the *Town-Ho* or by the *Jeroboam* (before she is taken over by the prophet Gabriel) than in an America like the *Pequod,* enlisted in a crazy crusade, an America in which the feudal or barbaric virtues are still strong. But it also says that a revolt in *Town-Ho* America is likely to be put down and, in that event, the available recourse for the defeated mutineers is to quit the ship. A culture both supplies and limits an artist's imagination. The America he knew presented Melville with no portents of a victorious proletarian revolution, and the variant of America he imagined in the *Pequod* portends only the common ruin of owners, officers, and crew.

A description of the *Pequod* that would draw attention to everything about her that illuminates the treatment of the theme of work in the novel must try to notice traits unique to her and traits she shares with all whale ships and even with all factories. To begin with a unique trait, she is the only ship whose name has associations with American history. The names of other American ships are connected with the sea and industry (the *Goney,* the *Town-Ho*) or derived from the Bible (the *Jeroboam,* the *Rachel*) or bespeak a ship's affluent and carefree independence (the *Bachelor*) or ironically depict her wretchedness (the *Delight*). The name Ahab's ship carries around the world is that of an exterminated New England Indian tribe. Her name thus evokes the blood-guilt of genocidal Puritan New England, the heartland of industrial capitalism in the New World. That the ship is chiefly owned and is managed by nominal, birthright Quakers does nothing to weaken her militant Puritan associations. These owners, Peleg and Bildad, and this owner-manager, Ahab, have fallen away from the pacifist principles of Quakerism. Because they are Nantucketers, whose outlook is shaped by participation in a bloody industry and perhaps in response to the mild traditions of their sect, they are among "the most sanguinary of all sailors and whale-hunters. They are fighting Quakers; they are Quakers with a vengeance" (16). In the characters of Bildad, Peleg, and Ahab it is disclosed that the *Pequod* is an enterprise possessed by a pious hypocrite and an uncouth bully and run by a cunning lunatic. The other owners are as powerless as the crew. They are "a crowd of old annuitants; widows, fatherless children, and chancery wards; each owning about the value of a timber head, or a foot of plank, or a nail or two of the ship. People in Nantucket invest their money in whaling vessels, the same way that you do yours in approved state stocks bringing in good interest."

The Puritan heritage of the *Pequod* is also evoked by her putting out to sea on Christmas Day, for Christmas is a holiday that lacks sanction in the Bible and so was regarded as just another working day by tradition-scorning Puritans. Her being under the command of a captain named for a ruler of the Northern Kingdom of Israel strengthens her association with the industrial and commercial North of the United States rather than with the country as a whole. In other ways, as will be seen, she is more a national than a regional symbol. Aboard the *Pequod* every needful thing that can be made out of the bones of her prey is carved out of whale ivory so that "tricked forth in the chased bones of her enemies" and named after other slaughtered enemies of her owners' forebears, the *Pequod* is a floating parable of death and destruction on the frontier of an expanding empire.

Among the traits that sets the *Pequod* off from other whalers is her age. She is older than most ships in the business and her age identifies her with the American ship of state. "She was a ship of the old school, rather small if anything; with an old fashioned claw-footed look about her." She had followed "the wild business of whaling . . . for more than half a century" (16). Her barbaric whale ivory decorations had been elaborated by Peleg, himself named for a post-deluge patriarch in Genesis. Side by side here are prehistoric and American historical associations for the ship. With respect to historical associations, the question should be asked: when was the *Pequod* launched? The answer is: fifty years before her final departure from Nantucket. But when was that? Melville is deliberately silent on that score because he wants to preserve the force of associations linking the *Pequod* to matters not limited to her nation and its history. Nevertheless, he supplies clues that lead to the conclusion that the date of the *Pequod*'s final departure from Nantucket is December 25, 1840. She sets sail in the year of a "Grand Contested Election for the Presidency of the United States" (1). Shortly before he joins the *Pequod*'s crew, Ishmael visits Father Mapple's chapel in New Bedford and inspects the cenotaphs of sailors lost at sea. The latest year to appear on a cenotaph is 1839. There is also an autobiographical clue. The whaling voyage of Herman Melville in the *Acushnet* began January 3, 1841. In this instance Melville is one of the makers of fiction who depart from the autobiographical just far enough to serve their literary purposes. So the building and the launching of the *Pequod* coincide with the making and adoption of the Constitution of 1787. Here the connotation of the *Pequod* is more national than New England.

The *Pequod* is not unique but is typical of American whale ships as a class in the social and ethnic composition of her crew. The *Pequod*'s crew is representative not just of the labor force of the whaling industry but of America's working class as it was in Melville's time and for many decades after that. It is preponderately an immigrant work force, supervised by the American born. The native minority of the sailors come from the farms and the forests; none are hereditary proletarians. As for most of the sailors

> not one in two of the many thousands of men before the mast employed in the American whale fishery, are American born, though pretty nearly all the officers are. Herein it is the same with the American whale fishery as with the American army and military and merchant navies, and the engineering forces employed in the construction of the American canals and railroads. . . . [T]he native America liberally supplies the brains, the rest of the world as generously supplies the muscle. (27)

(This generalization concerning the origins of the American working class does not mention the largely female and native-born work force of the New England textile mills. These workers are briefly on view in Melville's "The Tartarus of Maids.")

However, the whaling proletariat can be ethnically distinguished from the workers in other American industries. Aboard the *Pequod* "the harpooneers, with the great body of the crew, were a far more barbaric, heathenish, and motley set than any of the tame merchant-ship companies which my previous experiences had made me acquainted with." Ishmael attributes the strong representation in the crew of men from precapitalist cultures and regions "to the fierce uniqueness of the very nature of that wild Scandinavian vocation in which I had so abandonedly embarked" (28). "Wild Scandinavian" connotes bloody vikings gone berserk, and Ishmael's explanation suggests that the calling attracts men whose cultures have formed them to suit it. For those whose cultures have not, they abandon themselves when they embark. Ishmael is one of these. And elsewhere he suggests that the conditions of work in the industry uncivilize the civilized:

> Long exile from Christendom and civilization inevitably restores a man to that condition in which God placed him, *i.e.*, what is called savagery. Your true whale-hunter is as much a savage as an Iroquois. I myself am a savage, owing no allegiance but to the King of the Cannibals; and ready at any moment to rebel against him. (57)

So, in Ishmael's reflections on his work experience, there is a dialectical interdependence between personality and occupation, character and fate. The industry confirms some characters and transforms others.

In the *Pequod*'s cosmopolitan crew, fraternal solidarity between men of different races and white racist fear and hatred of nonwhites coexist. An analysis of the racial situation aboard the *Pequod* might begin with a description of the black contingent in her crew. There are three blacks aboard; that is, 10 percent of the work force are of African descent. This is not a circumlocution: only two of the three are Afro-Americans. The other is a native of Africa who shipped in a whaler off the West African coast and has never known slavery. The number of blacks is appropriate for a crew meant to be representative of the American working class. That one of the three is a skilled worker (or two, if the cook be classed as skilled) may not be so unlikely in pre-Civil War America, before the enactment of Jim Crow laws and the rise of lily-white unions.

The three are representative of the ages of man and of the range of psychological conditions of blacks in a racist society. There is the preadolescent ship keeper Pip, the harpooneer Dagoo, in the prime of life with "all his barbaric virtues" intact (27), and Fleece, the aged-weary, broken, shuffling cook. Comparisons among the three will further the description.

The difference between Fleece "as he was called" and Dagoo is the difference between an old man who has had to accommodate himself to racist oppression during a long life and a young man reared in a nonracist culture, never enslaved, and fortified in his self-esteem by his employment in a highly skilled, well-paying trade. An "imperial negro," Dagoo, "errect as a giraffe, moved about the decks in all the pomp of six feet five in his socks . . . a white man standing before him seemed a white flag come to beg truce of a fortress" (17). But when the ninety-year-old Fleece stands before a white man after "having been previously roused from his warm hammock at a most unseasonable hour" to broil a midnight whale steak for Stubb, the second mate, he "floundered along, and in obedience to the word of command, came to a dead stop . . . with both hands folded before him, and resting on his two-legged cane, he bowed his arched back till further over, at the same time inclining his head, so as to bring his best ear into play" (64). This is a typical Tomming stance, and though he cannot overtly resist, there remains in Fleece behind the mask of abject servility a hot spark of resentment at Stubb's humiliating treatment of him. Having served Stubb his whale steak and having been dismissed for the night with the order "Whale-balls for breakfast—don't forget," Fleece mutters, "Wish, by gor! whale eat him, 'stead of him eat whale." "I am bressed if he ain't more of shark dan Massa Shark hisself" (64).

The character of the ship keeper Pip is distinguished from Dagoo's and Fleece's in that Pip's character undergoes development in the novel. Pip is transformed from a sane and merry child into a schizoid because of his being thrust into work beyond his years and strength. Normally the job of a ship keeper is "to work the vessel while the boats are pursuing the whale." Most ship keepers are fully up to hunting whales, but not all are. Any crew member who is "unduly slender, clumsy, or timorous . . . is certain to be made a ship-keeper. It was so in the Pequod with the little negro Pippin by Nick-name, Pip by abbreviation" (93). But Stubb's after-oarsman sprains his hand and Pip has to replace him in Stubb's boat. They chase a whale and harpoon it:

> [A]s the fish received the darted iron, it gave its customary rap, which happened, in this instance, to be right under poor Pip's seat. The involuntary consternation of the moment caused him to leap, paddle in hand, out of the boat. . . . That instant the stricken whale started on a fierce run, the line swiftly straightened; and presto!

> poor Pip came all foaming up to the chocks of the boat, remorselessly dragged their by the line, which had taken several turns around his chest and neck.
>
> Tashtego stood in the bows. He was full of the fire of the hunt. He hated Pip for a paltroon. Snatching the boat-knife from its sheath, he suspended its sharp edge over the line, and turning toward Stubb, exclaimed interrogatively, "Cut?" Meantime Pip's blue, choked face plainly looked, Do, for God's sake!
>
> "Damn him, cut!" roared Stubb; and so the whale was lost and Pip was saved. (93)

(Pip's near-death in this episode anticipates in manner the deaths of Fedallah and Ahab at the end, just as his rescue in the next episode anticipates Ishmael's rescue at the end.)

No sooner does he catch his breath than Pip is "assailed by yells and execrations from the crew." He has equally offended Tashtego's barbaric joy in the hunt and the money-getting preoccupations of others. He is then "cursed . . . officially" by Stubb, who warns him: "Stick to the boat, Pip, or by the Lord, I won't pick you up if you jump; mind that. We can't afford to lose whales by the likes of you; a whale would sell for thirty times what you would, Pip, in Alabama!" Ishmael sees in this speech of Stubb's a hint that "man is a money-making animal which propensity too often interferes with his benevolence."

During another whale chase Pip jumps again and this time is left behind. "In three minutes, a whole mile of shoreless ocean was between Pip and Stubb." Stubb's abandonment of Pip is more careless than vindictive. He "did not mean to" leave Pip to drown. "Because there were two boats in his wake, and he supposed, no doubt, that they would of course come up to Pip very quickly, and pick him up." But the two other boats chase away after other whales. Pip treads water in isolation. "Out of the centre of the sea, poor Pip turned his crisp, curling black head to the sun, another lonely castaway. . . ." Pip orients himself as does a dying whale. Of Pip's isolation in nature Ishmael says "the awful lonesomeness is intolerable. The intense concentration of self in the middle of such heartless immensity, my God! who can tell it?" It parallels the social hierarchic isolation that helps madden Ahab. Pip is saved. "By the merest chance the ship at last rescued him; but from that hour the little negro went about the deck an idiot; such, at least, they said he was." He becomes a seer with a vision of "the joyous, heartless, ever-juvenile eternities." He sees divinity at work, "God's foot upon the treadle of the loom, and spoke it; and therefore his shipmates called him mad."

After that Pip is deprived of a personal identity. His very name belongs to a self that has perished. The old Manx sailor calls him by name and Pip responds: "Pip? who call ye Pip? Pip jumped from the whale-boat. Pip's missing.' " Asked by Ahab, " 'Who art thou, boy?' " he replies with an occupation, not with a name: " 'Bell-boy, sir; ship's crier; ding, dong, ding! Pip! Pip! Pip! One hundred pounds of clay reward for Pip; five feet high—looks cowardly—quickest known by that!' " (125). It is a parody of a runaway slave handbill. In another scene he dons the mask of Jim Crow: "And I, you, and he; and we, ye, and they, are all bats; and I'm a crow. Caw! caw! caw! caw! caw! caw! Ain't I a crow?" (99). Notice that the assumption of the Jim Crow role is predicated on the idea that everybody is batty. Pip's loss of identity releases his prophetic powers. He knows the *Pequod* is doomed and that no one on board will ever possess the gold doubloon nailed to her mainmast: " 'Ha, ha! old Ahab! the White Whale; he'll nail ye! . . . oh, the gold! the precious, precious gold!—the green miser'll hoard ye soon!" Parodying Stubb's ordering broiled whale steak from Fleece, he cries out, " 'Cook! ho, cook! and cook us!' " (99). The workers, not the object hunted and worked on, are the ultimate victims, who are ultimately cooked.

In Fleece and Pip, Ishmael sketches two possible lines of personality development for Afro-Americans. A black can either learn to survive by learning to shuffle before white tyrants or a black can go crazy. The ideal of a personality in which self-esteem is wedded to a demeanor of prideful composure would seem unlikely to be realized by blacks growing up in racist America and more likely to be realized by blacks like Dagoo growing up in a nonracist Africa and having a respected trade. But Pip was not made for work. His sensitivity and brightness are obstacles to his accommodation to the workaday world. In Ishmael's view black character encounters more difficulty in adjusting to that world than white, an observation he seeks to buttress with a comparison between Pip and the little "bread-faced steward" Dough-Boy, "the progeny of a bankrupt banker and a hospital nurse" (34). "In outer aspect, Pip and Dough-Boy made a match, like a black pony and a white one, of equal development, though of dissimilar color. . . . But while the hapless Dough-Boy was by nature dull and torpid in his intellects, Pip, though over tender-hearted, was at bottom very bright. . . . " (92). Although the steward's job of waiting table for the pagan harpooneers and Ahab provokes anxiety and fright in him, presumably the less-gifted white lad will find it easier to preserve his identity, his sanity, easier to endure an oppressive work experience.

It is conceivable that mid-nineteenth-century blacks observed by Melville showed stronger links with precapitalist modes of work and leisure than did contemporaneous whites. In any case he allows Ishmael to rhapsodize that blacks "ever enjoy all holidays and festivities with finer, freer relish than any other race. For blacks, the year's calendar should show naught but three hundred and sixty-five Fourth of Julys and New Year's Days." The only way such a generalization might be harmonized with the efficient work performance of Dagoo as harpooneer is by supposing that Dagoo is still psychologically in a precapitalist world where work and leisure are not contrasting states.

The *Pequod* is an American ship in which a racism normal to the country is manifest and in which an abnormal repudiation of racism is also manifest. Two episodes have just been referred to in which racist motivation in a character is strong. One is when Stubb, cruelly teasing Fleece, compels the ship's aged black cook to preach on brotherhood to a school of ravenous sharks as they attack the carcass of a whale lashed to the *Pequod*'s hull. The other is when Stubb, demonstrating his own practice of brotherhood, drives the child Pip crazy by abandoning him to sink or swim after Pip's second panicky leap from a whaleboat. In the first of these episodes the victimizer is at ease and the victim is at work. In the white man's idle hours the black must stand at attention or perform grotesque antics for the entertainment of his master. This is leisure-time racism. In the second episode victimizer and victim are both at work but at the moment of panic when the victim abandons the discipline of work, he himself is abandoned on the open ocean. This might be called an instance of workaday racism. The pursuit of the whale takes precedence over the saving of the child in the water because the whale is worth thirty times what the child is in the market, according to Stubb. Still another relation between victimizer and victim is presented in "Midnight, Forecastle" (40). It is an instance of racism within, not across, class lines and in which both victimizers and victims are at leisure.

A watch of the crew are "standing, lounging, leaning and lying in various attitudes," having just completed a period of work. As their replacements, the other watch, are summoned on deck, there is a little time for entertainment and a French Sailor proposes a jig.

> FRENCH SAILOR: There comes the other watch. Stand by all legs. Pip little Pip! hurrah with your tambourine!
>
> PIP *(Sulky and sleepy)*: Don't know where it is.
>
> FRENCH SAILOR: Beat thy belly, then, and wag thy ears. Jig it, men.

Pip here makes his first appearance in the novel as the reluctant black entertainer for sailors enjoying an interval between working and sleeping. About half the men dance to Pip's tambourine, after the Azores sailor pitches it up the scuttle to him. Among those who do not is Tashtego, the Indian harpooneer.

> FRENCH SAILOR: Merry-mad! Hold up thy hoop, Pip, till I jump through it.
>
> TASHTEGO *(Quietly smoking)*: That's a white man; he calls that fun: humph I save my sweat.

Tashtego does not belong to the world in which fun comes after work but to the world in which fun is integral to it. It is for the effort in which pleasure and duty are fused that he saves his sweat. He is as removed from the white man (capitalist man) at play as he is from the white man at work.

Now a storm blows up. The Old Manx Sailor points to a lurid streak of lightning in the sky, "all else pitch black."

> DAGOO: What of that? Who's afraid of black's afraid of me! I'm quarried out of it!
>
> SPANISH SAILOR *(Aside)*: He wants to bully, ah!—the old grudge makes me touchy. *(Advancing)* Aye, harpooneer, thy race is the undeniable dark side of mankind—devilish dark at that. No offense.
>
> DAGOO *(grimly)*: None.
>
> ....
>
> 5TH NANTUCKET SAILOR: What's that I saw—lightening? Yes.
>
> SPANISH SAILOR: No; Dagoo showing his teeth.

DAGOO *(springing)*: Swallow thine, mannikin! White skin, white liver!

SPANISH SAILOR *(meeting him)*: Knife thee heartily! big frame, small spirit!

ALL: A row! a row! a row!

So leisure-time racism within the crew progresses from the dance to the compelled music of Pip's tambourine, through the Spanish Sailor's racial slur, to a violent black-white confrontation. What keeps it within these limits is the necessity of managing the ship in the storm. A mate orders the hands back to duty in the rigging.

ALL: The squall! the squall! jump, my jollies! *(They scatter.)*

PIP: Jollies? Lord help such jollies! . . .

Ahad and Ishamel are the only two whites aboard the *Pequod* who are demonstrably uninvolved in the manifestations of racism in the ship. Ahab's only close associates are nonwhites—his Oriental harpooneer Fedallah and Pip. To his officers "socially, Ahab was inaccessible" (34). His attachment to Fedallah and Pip show Ahab's self-exile from capitalism's racial norms. He has transcended racism just as he has transcended the profit-taking life of service to the Nantucket market. Toward Fedallah Ahab's attitude is filial, even animal, subordination and toward Pip it is paternal protectiveness. In the Ahab-Fedallah relationship, however, appearances are otherwise: "Ahab seemed an independent lord; the Parsee but his slave" (129). This is the same illusion that deceives Captain Amasa Delano on board the *Saint Dominick* when he looks at, but does not see, the relationship between Don Benito Cereno and Babu, the leader of an insurrection of slaves in that Spanish ship. "But did you deeply scan him in his more secret confidential hours; when he thought no glance but one was on him; then you would have seen that even as Ahab's eyes so awed the crew's, the inscrutible Parsee's glance awed his." To Pip Ahab is bound as to a fellow victim of the misanthropic deities:

> There can be no hearts above the snow-line. Oh, ye frozen heavens! look down here. Ye did beget this luckless child, and have abandoned him, ye creative libertines. Here, boy; Ahab's cabin shall be Pip's home henceforth, while Ahab lives. Thou touches my inmost centre. . . . I feel prouder leading thee by thy black hand, than though I grasped an Emperor's! (135)

That Ahab is doomed is finally attested to by his attachment to Fedallah—it is stronger than his attachment to Pip. Pip, with the impulse to human solidarity he provokes, is the potential cure for Ahab's self-centered madness; Fedallah is the preserver of that madness. Ahab's character precludes his having a relationship of fraternal equality with anyone, of whatever race. In this he stands in contrast to Ishmael.

Ishmael's response to racism is one of growth and change and one that parallels Ahab's with Pip in that Queequeg saves him from his own impulse to self-destruction as Pip might have saved Ahab. In contrast to Ahab's relationships with Fedallah and Pip the Ishmael-Queequeg relationship is not a relationship of dominance and subordination but of equality.

Ishmael's relationship with Queequeg begins in anticipatory dread of sharing a bedroom with a "dark-complexioned" stranger who does not return to the Spouter Inn in New Bedford till late at night. Awaiting the stranger's arrival, "I rolled about a good deal, and could not sleep for a long time. At last I slid off into a light doze, and had pretty nearly made a good offing towards the land of Nod, when I heard a heavy footfall in the passage, and saw a glimmer of light come into the room under the door" (3). The "land of Nod" expresses the uncertainty of Ishmael's situation, the phrase connoting both sleep and the place of exile of the murderer Cain. Seeing the heavily tattooed Queequeg by the dim light of a candle, Ishmael hopes against hope that he is white. "I remembered the story of a white man—a whaleman too—who, falling among the cannibals, had been tattooed by them. I concluded that this harpooneer, in the course of his distant voyages, must have met with a similar adventure." But those portions of the stranger's skin not tattooed also seem "unearthly" to Ishmael. "To be sure, it might be nothing but a good coat of tropical tanning; but I never heard of a hot sun's tanning a white man into a purplish yellow one. However, I had never been to the South Seas; and perhaps the sun there produced these extraordinary effects upon the skin." Uncertain about Queequeg's racial identity and terror of his barbaric appearance prompts Ishmael to think of flight. "Had not the stranger stood between me and the door, I would have bolted out of it quicker than ever I bolted a dinner." When Queequeg, blowing out the candle and climbing into bed, discovers Ishmael there, he too feels threatened. "Who-e debel you?' he at last said—'you no speak-e, dam-me, I kill-e.' " But Queequeg's demeanor toward Ishmael, as soon as he learns that Ishmael is to be his bedmate, quickly changes to "not only a civil but a really kind and charitable" one, and Ishmael as quickly revises his attitude. "What's all this fuss I have been making about, thought I to myself—the man's a human being just as I am: he has just as much reason to fear me, as I have to be afraid of him. Better sleep with a sober cannibal than a drunken Christian." So Ishmael's fraternal impulses begin to prevail over his racist impulses. "I turned in, and never slept better in my life."

The fraternal relation that develops between Ishmael and Queequeg is a bond between self-sufficient equals. To Ishmael Queequeg "looked like a man who had never cringed and had never known a creditor" and like "George Washington cannibalistically developed" (10). Queequeg, this is to say, is a man unaccustomed to being dominated either by main force or by cash, a man fit to command in a struggle for independence. In an alien world Queequeg "seemed entirely at his ease; preserving the utmost serenity; content with his own companionship; always equal to himself" (10). Ishmael's association with Queequeg begins to disqualify him to be one of Ahab's subordinates in the insane pursuit of the White Whale, even before they embark on the *Pequod*. Ishmael and Queequeg, "a silent, solitary twain," sitting before the fire in the Spouter Inn, "the storm booming without in solemn swells," establish the closest of comradeships. "I felt a melting within me. No more my splintered heart and maddened hand were turned against the wolfish world. This soothing savage had redeemed it." The world has provoked Ishmael's desperate hostility, which tempts him to the thought of "deliberately stepping into the street, and methodically knocking people's hats off," which drives him to take to the sea as a substitute for suicide (1)—this world is redeemed for him, made a possible place to live in, by Queequeg's fraternal society. And this redemption of the world is one of Ishmael's inducements to declare his independence of the crusade compelled by the splintered heart and maddened hand of Ahab. "I'll try a pagan friend, thought I, since Christian kindness has proved but hollow courtesy."

"Christian kindness" has proved "hollow" to Ishmael in that he has suffered a social fall from the affluent, leisured world into which he was born into the poor and toilsome world of the proletariat where

> they rather order me about some, and make me jump from spar to spar, like a grasshopper in a May meadow. . . . It touches one's sense of honor, particularly if you come of an old established family in the land, the Van Rensselaers, or Randolphs, or Hardicanutes. And more than all, if just previous to putting your hand into the tar-pot, you have been lording it as a country schoolmaster, making the tallest boys stand in awe of you. The transition is a keen one, I assure you, from a schoolmaster to a sailor, and requires a strong decoction of Seneca and the Stoics to enable you to grin and bear it. (1)

Though not a Van Rensselaer, Melville was descended from "an old established family" of Hudson Valley patrons, the Gansevorts, on his mother's side; his grandfather, Thomas Melville, had been a major in the Continental Army during the Revolution. And Melville—after Allan Melville, his father, oppressed by debts and out of his mind, died in 1832—had to go to work at the age of twelve. His last job before going to sea in the whaler *Achusnet* was as a country schoolmaster. Thus Ishmael shares with his author a history of displacement, disinheritance, alienation. Such keen transitions downward can sharpen the eyes of a narrator who peers into the class structure of society. When the ground on which one stands gives way, what can be taken for granted? So Ishmael takes leave of the land to stand upon the sea, "having little or no money in my purse" (1). This lightness of purse functions as nemesis in American tragedies. If Ishmael is not the victim ultimately but the observer and reporter of tragedy it is partly due to the bond he forms with Queequeg.

Queequeg accepts Ishmael's offer of friendship only when he is persuaded that it is not meant casually but for keeps. Then everything is shared between them. "He seemed to take to me quite as naturally and unbiddenly as I to him . . . and said that henceforth we were married; meaning in his country's phrase, that we were bosom friends; he would gladly die for me, if need should be" (10). Some readers have chosen to take such passages as declarations of homosexual love, but readers who entertain the possibility of human solidarity not limited in form and scope to the sexual need not restrict themselves to that interpretation. In this discussion the importance of the passage is that it makes a stage in Ishmael's emancipation from his cultural heritage of racism and that the linking of Ishmael and Queequeg does not arise from but precedes their experience of working together. Because of their mutual affection

Queequeg decides to go to Nantucket with Ishmael, "ship aboard the same vessel, get into the same watch, the same boat, the same mess with me," but for Ishmael there is a practical advantage in this joint venture too, "for besides the affection I now felt for Queequeg, he was an experienced harpooneer, and as such, could not fail to be of great usefulness to one, who, like me, was wholly ignorant of the mysteries of whaling." (12). Racism is frequently exacerbated in the competition for jobs among workers; between the skilled Queequeg and the unskilled Ishmael there can be no competition.

The next stage in Ishmael's transcendence of racism is the public manifestation of his friendship with Queequeg. They leave the Spouter Inn together, borrow a wheelbarrow, and cart their belongings to the *Moss,* which will carry them from New Bedford to Nantucket. "As we were going along the people stared; not at Queequeg so much—for they were used to seeking cannibals like him in their street,—but at seeing him and me upon such confidential terms. But we heeded them not, going along wheeling the barrow by turns." (13). Aboard the *Moss* they share an intoxicating experience of the wild, free, traditionaless open sea. "How I snuffed the Tartar air!—how I spurned the turnpike earth!—that common highway all over dented with the marks of slavish heels and hoofs; and turned to admire the magnanimity of the sea which will permit no records." Ishmael here links the Golden Horde galloping over the roadless steppes to the little schooner bouncing over rough water and contrasts them to civilized humanity and beasts of burden whose common lot is to be mired in tradition, domesticated to accept a slavish subordination in the workaday world. "At the same foam-fountain, Queequeg seemed to drink and reel with me." But the other passengers on the *Moss* do not share in the intoxicating feeling of liberation that seizes Ishmael and Queequeg. Instead they evince their customary racism. "So full of this reeling scene were we, as we stood by the plunging bowsprit, that for some time we did not notice the jeering glances of the passengers, a lubber-like assembly, who marvelled that two fellow beings should be so companionable; as though a white man were anything more dignified than a white-washed negro." This scene announces a paradox that recurs throughout the novel. On the one hand "the sea which permits no records" is the epitome of spontaneity and freedom; on the other hand, to be at sea is to be in the presence of people who bring to the sea all the baggage of civilization, its traditions, its iron necessities of discipline—it is to be imprisoned in floating metaphors of the patriarchal family, the state, the factory.

Ishmael characterizes the whale ship as a frontier phenomenon, "the pioneer in ferreting out the remotest and least known parts of the earth" which "first interpreted between [American and European men-of-war] and the savages" (24). The floating factories of youthful capitalism are also the forerunners of its imperialist expansion. But it is what goes on in the ship that must stay at the center of this discussion. In the *Pequod* fraternal democracy and rigid dictatorship are deeply intertwined. This unity of opposites is strikingly exhibited in the dining routines of the *Pequod*'s officers and harpooneers.

The harpooneers are privileged workers. Among their privileges is that they share the rations of the officers rather than those of the seamen before the mast. First the officers eat at the captain's table, then the harpooneers. The painful table etiquette of the captain and his mates is in stark contrast to the democratic revelry infusing the table manners of the harpooneers. The officers go to dinner in the captain's cabin one by one, in descending order of rank; each mate approaches the table only after his superior is seated. Departure from dinner is in reverse order of rank. Third mate

> Flask was the last person down to dinner, and Flask is the first man up. Consider! For hereby Flask's dinner was badly jammed in point of time. Starbuck and Stubb both had the start of him; and they also have the privilege of lounging in the rear. If Stubb even, who is but a peg higher than Flash, happens to have but a small appetite, and soon shows symptoms of concluding his repast, then Flask must bestir himself, he will not get more than three mouthfuls that day; for it is against holy usage for Stubb to precede Flask to the deck. (34)

Poor Flask has never really had a square meal aboard ship since he became an officer, and Ishmael philosophizes: "There's the fruits of promotion now; there's the vanity of glory; there's the insanity of life!" The social atmosphere at the officers' mess is oppressive. Their "solemn meals" are eaten "in awful silence; and yet at table old Ahab forbade not conversation; only he himself was dumb." Apparently none of the mates is tempted to set table talk going. "What a relief it was to choking Stubb, when a rat made a sudden racket in a hole below." Sailors "going aft at dinnertime to get a peek at Flask through the cabin sky-light" would see him "sitting silly and dumbfounded before awful Ahab."

The atmosphere changes when the officers leave and the steward Dough-Boy resets the table for the harpooneers.

> In strange contrast to the hardly tolerable constraint and nameless invisible domineerings of the captain's table, was the entire care-free license and ease, the almost frantic democracy of those inferior fellows the harpooneers. While their masters, the mates, seemed afraid of the sound of the hinges of their own jaws, the harpooneers chewed their food with such relish that there was a report to it. They dined like lords; they filled their bellies like Indian ships all day loading with spices.

Living and dining in the captain's cabin the barbarian harpooneers enjoy the material privileges of the officers without suffering the deprivation of freedom and spontaneity that comes with membership in the ruling hierarchy of the ship. They are skilled workers who have been able to keep a vital part of the precapitalist world that shaped them. They are not, however, above enjoying browbeating the steward Dough-Boy in a manner reminiscent of Stubb's treatment of Fleece (64). Tashtego speeds up the steward's table waiting by jabbing him with a fork and (playfully) threatening to scalp him. Dagoo asks for another helping by "thrusting his head into a great empty wooden trencher, while Tashtego, knife in hand, began laying out the circle preliminary to scalping him." Meanwhile, Queequeg appears to the terrified Dough-Boy to be on the point of reversion to cannibalism. "Alas! Dough-Boy! hard fares the white waiter who waits on cannibals." The tension between hierarchy and fraternity, dictatorship and democracy, presented dramatically in "The Cabin-Table," is generalized in "The Specksnyder":

> Through the long period of a Southern whaling voyage (by far the longest of all voyages now or ever made by man), the peculiar perils of it, and the community of interest prevailing among a company, all of whom, high or low, depend for their profits, not upon fixed wages, but upon their common luck, together with their common vigilance, intrepidity, and hard work; though all these things do in some cases tend to beget a less rigorous discipline than in merchantmen generally; yet, never mind how much like an old Mesopotamian family

> these whalemen may, in some primitive instance, live together; for all that, the punctilious externals, at least, of the quarterdeck are seldom materially relaxed, and in no instance done away with. Indeed, many are the Nantucket ships in which you will see the skipper . . . extorting almost as much outward homage as if he wore the imperial purple. (33)

The *Pequod* is no "primitive instance" of fraternity aboard a whale ship. In her commander's brain "sultanism became incarnate in an irresistible dictatorship" (33). The *Pequod*'s crew, except Ishmael, has been "picked and packed by fate" (41) to submit to that dictatorship. Melville links the fate of the *Pequod*'s crew and the deliverance of Ishmael from that fate to the work they do and how they do it.

As in all ships in the whaling business, in the *Pequod* the work of the crew, except for that of the maintenance men like the Carpenter, the Blacksmith, and the Cook, is governed by the chance of the hunt. The rhythm of work is characteristically a short pulse of intense, dangerous labor as the workers kill and butcher a whale, render its blubber, store whale oil in casks, and clean up the mess. Between these short pulses are alternate longer periods of leisurely amusement and preparations for the chase accompanied by daydreaming, meditation, hallucination, and sleep. These longer periods of relaxed activity are dangerous politically and physically. In most industries capitalists are inclined to lay off workers when there is no profitable labor at hand for the workers to perform. This practice not only saves money but counteracts the explosive agitational possibilities inherent in the concentration of unemployed proletarians in a factory.

This practice is not available in the whaling industry. Once a ship is out to sea, the possibility of dismissing the crew, or even part of the crew, is slim. The seamen are close to irreplaceable, and when men jump ship in Polynesia the hunt for substitutes is a costly waste of time. The floating factory must maintain the number of hands needed for full production during periods when there is no production at all. Much of the time, the whale ship will appear, from the capitalist viewpoint, to be "overmanned" but there is no remedy for the situation. The *Pequod* is a ship filled with men who have the leisure to think over the meaning of Ahab's enterprise and weigh the question whether their commander's interests and their own coincide.

Ahab understands this political danger. He had "perhaps somewhat prematurely" announced to the crew that his only interest is in the pursuit and capture of a single whale. "It might be that a long interval would elapse ere the White Whale was seen. During that long interval Starbuck would ever be apt to fall into open rebellion against his captain's leadership . . . when they stood their long night watches, his officers and men must have some nearer things to think of than Moby-Dick" (46). Ahab's manipulative tactical defense against the danger of revolt is to chase every whale that comes in view, to keep the crew busy with "the natural, nominal purpose of the Pequod's voyage; observe all customary usages; and not only that, but force himself" to show "interest in the general pursuit of his profession." To the self-made Ahab, free of the influence of the Nantucket market, "the permanent constitutional condition of manufactured man . . . is sordidness." He will make that condition serve an interest that is its negation. "I will not strip these men, thought Ahab, of all hopes of cash." Deprived of that hope they might revolt without fear of punishment, for Ahab, in revealing the true purpose of his cruise, had "laid himself open to the unanswerable charge of usurpation; and with perfect impunity, both moral and legal, his crew, if so disposed, and to that end competent, could refuse all further obedience to him, and even violently wrest from him the command." Against revolt Ahab finds in the routines of work and the normal expectations of reward an ally.

The long periods of relaxed activity between whale captures include duties physically dangerous to the men. Easy monotony makes going to sleep on the job a hazard to life for a sailor aboard the *Pequod* when on lookout at the masthead or at the helm when the ship is in quiet waters. Ishmael himself falls asleep at the masthead—at the risk of his own life—and at the helm—at the risk of the lives of the entire crew. As lookout from the foremast Ishmael describes the infectious sleepiness overcoming the workers assigned to that undemanding job: "Ere forgetfulness altogether overcame me, I had noticed that the seamen at the main and mizen mast-heads were already drowsy. So that at last all three of us lifelessly swung from the spars, and for every swing that we made there was a nod below from the slumbering helmsman" (61).

He himself is the slumbering helmsman in another episode. A sense of disorientation overtakes him as he stands at the *Pequod*'s tiller in the night watch and observes his shipmates rendering blubber in the try-pots:

> Wrapped, for that interval, in darkness myself, I but better saw the redness, the madness, the ghastliness of others. The continual sight of the fiend shapes before me, capering half in smoke and half in fire, these at last begat a kindred vision in my soul, so soon as I began to yield to that unaccountable drowsiness which ever would come over me at a midnight helm.
>
> But that night, in particular, a strange (and ever since inexplicable) thing occurred to me. Starting from a brief standing sleep, I was horribly conscious of something fatally wrong. The jaw-bone of the tiller smote my side, which leaned against it; in my ears was the low hum of the sails, just beginning to shake in the wind; I thought my eyes were open; I was half-conscious of putting my fingers to the lids and mechanically stretching them still further apart. . . . Uppermost was the impression that whatever swift, rushing thing I stood on was not so much bound to any haven ahead as rushing from all havens astern. . . . Convulsively my hand grasped the tiller, but with the crazy conceit that the tiller was, somehow, in some enchanted way, inverted. My God! what is the matter with me? thought I. Lo! in my brief sleep I had turned myself about, and was fronting the ship's stern, with my back to her prow and the compass. In an instant I faced back, just in time to prevent the vessel from flying up into the wind, and very probably capsizing her. How glad and grateful the relief from this unnatural hallucination of the night. (96)

Sudden wakefulness not only frees Ishmael from hallucination but rescues him from destruction.

Whether the narcotic effect is provided at the masthead by soft winds over the sunny pastoral ocean or at the helm by the spectacle of the frenzied sweating night labors of seamen around the infernal try-pots, going to sleep on the job brings Ishmael the sleeper to terror at the edge of annihilation. Standing asleep at the masthead, "move your foot or hand an inch; slip your hold at all; and your identity comes back in horror. . . . Perhaps, at mid-day, in the fairest weather, with one half-throttled shriek you drop through that transparent air into the summer sea, no more to rise forever" (35). The salvation of the sleeping masthead lookout is to be roused to wakefulness by the sighting of a whale: "Suddenly bubbles seemed bursting beneath my closed eyes; like vices my hands grasped the shrouds; some invisible gracious agency preserved me; with a shock

I came back to life. And lo! close under our lee, not forty fathoms off, a gigantic Sperm Whale lay rolling in the water. . . . As if struck by some enchanter's wand, the sleepy ship and every sleeper in it all at once started into wakefulness" (61). Here the preserving gracious agency is the call to the whale hunt, but in the try-works episode Ishmael's observation of the work in progress is the agency of near disaster. Watching the work disorients Ishmael, causing him to cease to function as a helmsman. The salvation of the sleeping Ishmael at the helm is in his timely ability to be aware of "something fatally wrong" and in his "half-conscious" effort to increase his awareness, "putting my fingers to the lids and mechanically stretching them still further apart." When he is entranced by nature at the masthead, the call to work awakens Ishmael; when he is fascinated and repelled at the helm by the labors around the try-works and having unconsciously turned his back on those labors, his terrifying loss of orientation jars him awake.

Another somnolent work experience is the mat making in which Ishmael cooperates with Queequeg. As so often with Thoreau, physical labor provides Ishmael a foundation for philosophical meditation. The two friends seem to be the only men aboard the *Pequod* who are at all active or making any noise. "[T]he seamen were lazily lounging about the decks, or vacantly gazing into the lead-colored waters. Queequeg and I were mildly employed weaving what is called a sword-mat . . . each silent sailor seemed resolved into his own invisible self." The labors of the two men working are not synchronized—Ishmael's movements are regular and Queequeg's random. "As I kept passing and repassing the filling or woof or marline between the long yarns of the warp, using my own hand for the shuttle, and as Queequeg, standing sideways, ever and anon slid his heavy oaken sword between the threads, and idly looking off upon the water, carelessly and unthinkingly drove home every yarn" (47). Ishmael makes of this work experience a metaphor for the interplay in the world of necessity, free will, and chance—necessity represented by the immovable woof, free will by the regularly moving shuttle, and chance by the randomly tamping sword. His meditation is interrupted by a call from the masthead to a whale hunt "so strange, long drawn, and musically wild and unearthly, that the ball of free will dropped from my hand." Not only is his free will relinquished at the call from the masthead but the work of mat-making must be set aside in behalf of that higher embodiment of necessity and chance, the whale hunt.

Ishmael's tendency to philosophize, induced by mat-making, is not indulged at the risk of physical danger as is his tendency to sleep at the masthead or the helm. In contrast to all these easy-going jobs are the relentless exhausting tasks immediately associated with the capture of whales and the manufacture of whale oil. While engaged in these tasks there is little opportunity for sleep or philosophy:

> [M]any is the time, when, after the severest uninterrupted labors, which knew no night; continuing straight through for ninety-six hours; when from the boat, where they have swelled their wrists with all day rowing on the Line,—they only step to the deck to carry vast chains, and heave the heavy windlass, and cut and slash, yea, and in their vary sweatings to be smoked and burned anew by the combined fires of the equatorial sun and the equatorial try-works; when on the heel of all this, they have finally bestirred themselves to cleanse the ship, and make a spotless dairy-room of it, many is the time the poor fellows, just buttoning the necks of their clean frocks, are startled by the cry "There she blows!" and away they fly to fight another whale, and go through the whole weary thing again. Oh! my friends, but this is man-killing! Yet this is life. (98)

Exhausted by man-killing labor, losing himself in the interspersed periods of leisurely, undemanding duties, Ishmael oscillates between trying to stay alive and preserve his identity and courting annihilation and oblivion. His going to sea is a substitute for suicide. Like the *Pequod*'s Carpenter Perth, he belongs to a class of men whose social ruin impels them to take ship.

> [T]o the death-longing eyes of such men, who still have in them some interior compunctions against suicide, does the all-contributed and all-receptive ocean alluringly spread forth his whole plain of unimaginable, taking terrors, and wonderful, new-life adventures; and from the hearts of infinite Pacifics, the thousand mermaids sing to them—"Come hither, brokenhearted; here is another life without guilt of intermediate death; here are wonders supernatural, without dying for them—"Come hither, hither! bury thyself in a life which, to your now equally abhorred and abhorring, landed world, is more oblivious than death. (112)

But with this identity of situation and outlook toward the sea between Ishmael and Perth there are also important contrasts. These relate to the burden of guilt, the kind of work done, and the way it is performed.

The ruin of Ishmael is the ruin of an orphan in the transition from patroon to proletarian, from schoolmaster to deckhand. Ishmael receives his ruin as the burden of an innocent victim maliciously tormented by a sadistic providence. (This aspect of his condition allows him to empathize with Ahab.) His sense of wronged innocence enters into his choice and style of work. The ruin of Perth, in contrast, is the ruin of an irresponsible parent who had destroyed his wife and children through his addiction to alcohol. Perth therefore receives his ruin as an incurred guilt. His skilled and steady work at the *Pequod*'s forge is penitential. "No murmur, no impatience, no petulance did come from him. Silent, slow, and solemn; bowing over still further his chronically broken back, he toiled away, as if toil were life itself, and the heavy beating of his hammer the heavy beating of his heart" (112).

By contrast Ishmael's work is not skilled, not steady, not penitential. He early justifies his preference for unskilled work: "I abominate all honorable, respectable toils, trials, and tribulations of every kind whatsoever. It is quite as much as I can do to take care of myself," says Ishmael to explain why he would rather go to sea as a simple sailor than as a "Commodore, or a Captain, or a Cook" (1). He does not like being ordered about (the common lot of sailors), but he would rather endure subordination than have to tell other people what to do like a ship's commander. And to be a cook or carpenter or blacksmith is constantly to have to meet the demands of the officers and crew. The ruin of his family and his attitude toward that ruin determine his choice of a job and manner of working at it. Innate character perhaps contributes to that determination. At any event, Ishmael has an irrepressible, or at least unrepressed, need for leisure—a need that captains and cooks and other specialists must learn to repress in themselves. In the *Pequod* and in all "overmanned" whalers the leisurely, prehistoric "wonderful patience of industry" that produces scrimshaw carving (57) is beyond the grasp of the specialists who are constantly at the beck and call of others, even in the intervals between the frenzied chases after profits and revenge. Cruising on a vessel that becomes a metaphor for industrializing America and whose business provides the matter of a national epic, Ishmael needs the leisure to become its sailor-bard inspired by the muse equality. He and his alter ego, the Melville who had to milk the cows every morning before putting his goose quill to the manuscript of *Moby-Dick*'s draft of a draft cry out in one voice, "Oh, Time, Strength, Cash, and Patience!" (32). Such is his longing for conditions making possible fully enjoyed leisure. Given his needs his choice of work is rational. The *Pequod,* however, is under the dictatorship of a man who does not need and does not want to need leisure. Ahab is above all others the man in the study of whom Ishmael can define his own approach to work and leisure.

A paradox of Ahab is that he has everything to do with the tragedy of the *Pequod* and next to nothing to do with the business of whaling. At his first appearance on deck he strikes Ishmael as an idle supernumerary in the ship's company, a man without discernible function. "[F]or all that he said, or perceptibly did, on the at last sunny deck, he seemed as unnecessary there as another mast" (18). Later Ahab will force himself to take a part in the ordinary business of the cruise but only as a precaution against losing his authority over the crew. But in his every waking moment Ahab is preoccupied with his special work, the vengeful assault on the White Whale. Human distractions from that purpose he quite easily puts aside. That ease he has bought by a total estrangement from the world. To live always for his vengeful work he must be damned. Of the golden Pacific sunset, which ends the day on which he has summoned the crew to his monomaniac crusade against Moby-Dick, Ahab says, "This lovely light, it lights not me; all loveliness is anguish to me, since I can ne'er enjoy" (37). He can perceive but not enjoy the beauty of the world because he has been "damned, most subtly and malignantly! damned in the midst of Paradise!" He has been seduced by a subtle and malignant beast into regarding the "enjoying power," which he lacks, as "low." His damnation is his willingness to commit himself to work like a fiend at his special calling. The "cautious comprehensiveness and unloitering vigilance with which Ahab threw his brooding soul into this unfaltering hunt" is fiendish (44). From the hunt there is no escape, not even in sleep. Ahab "sleeps with clenched hands; and wakes with his own bloody nails in his palms" because at night he is ridden by exhausting and intolerable dreams" of his vengeful work. Sometimes "accursed fiends beckoned him to leap down among them; when this hell in himself yawned beneath him, a wild cry would be heard through the ship; and with glaring eyes Ahab would burst from his state room, as though escaping from a bed that was on fire." In Ishmael's analysis Ahab's sleepwalking exhibits the deep split in him between the involuntary tendency toward life and the willed commitment to accursed work, between an impulse toward sanity and a cunning madness. And Ishmael prays for him: "God help thee, old man, thy thoughts have created a creature in thee."

What Ishmael wills and does not will is the opposite of what Ahab wills and does not will. Ahab, living for his vengeful work, strips himself of his impulse to human solidarity (except in his strictly self-controlled relationship to Pip) and becomes a whirring vengeance-machine who can say of his relationship to the crew "my one cogged circle fits into all their various wheels, and they revolve" (37). Mastered by his chosen work, he is incapable of leisure. Ishmael is the only master of leisure (and of work) aboard the *Pequod.* He is less subject to vengefulness and to dollars than any others.

Leisure and a leisurely style of working afford Ishmael opportunities to save himself in study and enjoyment of the world. His work experiences at the masthead, at the tiller, and in mat-making have been considered. His style of work orients him away from Ahab and toward living in a fraternal relation to humanity. Standing at the masthead, he is in a rapturous (though dangerous) unity with nature, which contrasts with Ahab's damning total separation from nature in the "Sunset" soliloquy. Standing at the tiller and watching his shipmates rendering blubber in the try-pots, he involuntarily turns his back on that energy-consuming, life-burning industrial process—coming back to himself in a disorienting trance (as opposed to Ahab, who tries to escape from himself in sleep). Making a sword mat with Queequeg, he finds in the work and in his and Queequeg's styles of work a means of making philosophical sense of a world of necessity, free will, and chance.

Another work experience with Queequeg stimulates Ishmael's philosophizing. Queequeg is working on the back of a whale lashed to the hull. "So down there, some ten feet below the level of the deck, the poor harpooneer flounders about, half on the whale's back, half in the water" (72). Queequeg faces two dangers as he works to insert a blubber hook in the whale's back: he risks being jammed between the ship and the whale as both pitch and roll in the tossing sea, and he risks slipping off the whale's back into the school of frenzied sharks that are attacking the carcass. To guard him from these dangers is the duty of Ishmael. The means is the monkey-rope. It is made "fast to Queequeg's broad canvas belt, and fast to my narrow leather one . . . and should poor Queequeg sink to rise no more, then both usage and honor demanded, that instead of cutting the cord, it should drag me down in his wake." Ishmael stands on the side of the ship and occasionally jerks Queequeg out of a jam between whale and ship or away from the mouths of sharks. The monkey-rope has connotations of subservience and dependency arising from its reference to the organ-grinder and his monkey, but the organ-grinder is not tied to the monkey and aboard the *Pequod* the monkey-rope becomes a symbol of human interdependency. "I seemed distinctly to perceive that my own individuality was now merged in a joint stock company of two: that my free will had received a mortal wound; and that another's misfortune might plunge innocent me into unmerited disaster and death."

The *Pequod*'s way of using the monkey-rope is unique in the industry. "The monkey-rope is found in all whalers; but it was only in the Pequod that the monkey and his holder were ever tied together." Something much like a true monkey-rope, however, appears in the relationship of Ahab and Starbuck. Desiring to stand lookout for Moby-Dick, Ahab arranges to be hauled up to the main masthead. His "monkey holder" in this episode is Starbuck. Ahab, "settling his firm relying eye upon the chief mate, said,—'Take this rope, sir—I give it into thy hands, Starbuck.' Then arranging his person in the basket, he gave word for them to hoist him to his perch, Starbuck being the one who secured the rope at last; and afterwards stood near it" (130). This is more a true monkey-rope than the one attaching Queequeg and Ishmael because it sets up a relationship of dependency, not interdependency. Starbuck could let the rope slip out of his hands without physical danger to himself but with disastrous results for Ahab. Letting slip the rope would be an easy means of physical salvation for Starbuck and the ship's crew; their doom is in submission to Ahab. That Ahab is momentarily in Starbuck's hands is only literally true. More closely considered the rope in this episode betokens Starbuck's utter subservience to

Ahab. This is no joint stock company of two. Independent Ahab knows he can depend on Starbuck to cooperate in his own destruction. Ishmael and Queequeg know they can depend on each other to collaborate for mutual preservation.

Ishmael brings curiosity and the impulse to play to his work. These elements govern his natural working pace. Early in the narrative, for instance, when the *Pequod* weighs anchor off Nantucket, Ishmael is pushing the capstan that is hauling up the anchor. In this conspicuous position he tries to work at his natural pace, that is, to take it easy, to pause and think about the wisdom of what he is doing, to look curiously at his surroundings and to comment on them to his fellow worker Queequeg. This dawdling gets him a swift kick in the rear from Peleg, one of the *Pequod*'s owners and a man who is paying Ishmael for his labor power, not his curiosity. But when Ishmael works at scrubbing out the try-pot, he enjoys freedom from supervision, which is not usually available to workers. He takes advantage of his position. It is hard for a supervisor to see what a man inside a large iron pot is doing. It is therefore a place for rest, sociability, and learning as well as work. "During the night-watches some cynical old sailors will crawl into the try-pots and coil themselves away there for a nap. While employed in polishing them—one man in each pot, side by side—many confidential communications are carried on there, over the iron lips." Ishmael himself, the curious investigator of the natural world, finds the try-pot a place "for profound mathematical meditations. It was in the left hand try-pot of the Pequod, with soapstone diligently circling about me, that I was indirectly struck by the remarkable fact that, in geometry all bodies gliding along the cycloid, my soapstone for example, will descend from any point in precisely the same time" (96). In Ishmael's style of working, the soapstone is diligent, not its manipulator. Expending a minimum amount of elbow grease, he lets gravity do the work. Curious and easygoing, he approaches the work of scouring the pot more as a game than as a job to be accomplished speedily and efficiently; and the game turns into a scientific experiment testing the acceleration of gravity. Like Thoreau, Ishmael would earn his bread without working up a sweat, and he gains increased knowledge of the laws of nature as the indirect product of the work experience. That is the memorable reward of his style of working. No profit-minded foreman would stand for Ishmael's studious soldiering on the job while inside the try-pot if he could see what was going on there.

And no time-study engineer would approve of how Ishmael conducts himself in a circle of sailors who sit on the deck around a tub of crystallized sperm oil that must be kneaded back into liquid form.

> As I sat there at my ease, cross-legged on the deck; after the bitter exertion at the windlass; under a blue tranquil sky; the ship under indolent sail, and gliding serenely along; as I bathed my hands in those soft, gentle globules of infiltrated tissues, woven almost within the hour; as they richly broke into my fingers, and discharged all their opulence, like fully ripe grapes their wine; as I snuffed up that uncontaminated aroma,—literally and truly like the smell of spring violets; I declare to you, that for the time I lived as in a musky meadow; I forgot all about our horrible oath; in that inexpressible sperm, I washed my hands and heart of it. (94)

To forget the horrible oath is to be freed from thralldom to Ahab. Ishmael's emancipation from Ahab happens when he is at his ease, having just been released from "bitter exertion." The weather is benign and the ship is lazing along "under indolent sail." The feel and smell of the work is supremely agreeable in contrast to his experience of work around the try-works—the searing heat from scalding pots and the smoke from the burning whale, "horrible to inhale, and inhale it you must, and not only that, but you must live in it for the time" (96). When he absolves himself of his oath to Ahab, the work Ishmael is engaged in is cooperative. "I squeezed that sperm till a strange sort of insanity overcame me; and I found myself unwittingly squeezing my co-laborers hands in it, mistaking their hands for the gentle globules. Such an abounding, affectionate, friendly, loving feeling did this avocation beget; that at last I was continually squeezing their hands, and looking into their eyes sentimentally." Ishmael's insanity here is the opposite of Ahab's. It is an insanity of species unity, of individual selflessness, and is engendered in a form of work that is not work but "avocation." It evokes one of Ishmael's invocations: "Come; let us squeeze hands all round; nay, let us all squeeze ourselves into each other." Ahab's insanity, by contrast, is an insanity of selfishness characterized by Ahab's regarding himself as the sole representative of humanity and regarding others as mere manufactured men, the tools of his will. It is engendered in a form of work from which any element of avocation is absent. It is a permanent, not like Ishmael's momentary, insanity.

Ishmael's way of working is good for his physical and his spiritual health; its tempo helps preserve his body and mind. He is distinguished in this way from his bosom companion Queequeg and from Ahab. Crazy Ahab works in a way that declares and sustains his madness. Queequeg is compelled to work himself nearly to death. Exhausting, sickening work is part of his normal duties as a harpooneer; dangerous, maddening toil is voluntarily undertaken by Ahab:

> Be it said, that in this vocation of whaling, sinecures are unknown; dignity and danger go hand in hand; till you get to be Captain, the higher you rise the harder you toil. So with poor Queequeg, who as harpooner, must not only face all the rage of the living whale, but—as we have elsewhere seen—mount his dead back in a rolling sea; and finally descend into the gloom of the hold, and bitterly sweating all day in that subterraneous confinement, resolutely handle the clumsiest casks and see to their stowage. (110)

Out of the larger context of the novel, Ishmael's assertion about the captain's work is ambiguous. It can mean that the captain works harder than his subordinates or it can mean that once a man attains a captaincy, his rise in the hierarchy no longer carries harder work as its concomitant. Ahab is totally absorbed in his work, whose ends have not been defined for him by the owners or by the capitalist system but by himself alone. He wills himself to be the hardest-working man on board the *Pequod.* But had Ahab allowed his performance to be governed by the interests of the owners and the system, he would have limited himself to strictly managerial functions instead of taking an active hand in the whale hunt and the preparation of his own hunting equipment, the forging of his harpoon, for example (113). In giving him command of the *Pequod* it was not the intent of the owners to provide Ahab with a sinecure but neither did they intend to give him an assignment in which "dignity and danger go hand in hand." They intended to give him the dignity without the danger. They expected him not to participate in whale hunts, for that would be an insane risk for a one-legged man to take. To hide from the owners his inclination to take insane risks, Ahab smuggles aboard the extra men who will be his boat crew.

About the working conditions of Queequeg there is no ambiguity. Much more work is gotten out of this skilled man than out of his unskilled companion Ishmael. The work that is hardest on Queequeg's health is in the ship's hold stowing casks of oil. It is an emergency job, a result of the discovery of an oil leak from the casks. When Starbuck reports this to Ahab, the response is "Let it leak!" Starbuck protests:

> "What will the owners say, sir?"
>
> "Let the owners stand on Nantucket beach and outyell typhoons. What cares Ahab? Owners, owners? Thou art always prating to me, Starbuck, about those miserly owners, as if the owners were my conscience. But look ye, the only real owner of anything is its commander." (109)

This is the last overt confrontation in the novel between the motives of profit and vengeance. Starbuck objects that if the leak is not stopped, the ship will lose "in one day more oil than we may make good in a year. What we come twenty thousand miles to get is worth saving, sir."

> "So it is, so it is; if we can get it."
>
> "I was speaking of the oil in the hold, sir."
>
> "And I was not speaking or thinking of that at all."

But Ahab quickly reconsiders his response. Probably in accordance with his policy of not depriving his crew members of their hope of cash, he accedes to Starbuck's request that the oil leak be searched for and plugged. While working at this job Queequeg takes ill. Ishmael sees him at work in the hold "where, stripped to his woolen drawers, the tattooed savage was crawling about amid that dampness and slime, like a green lizard at the bottom of a well. And a well, or an ice-house, it somehow proved to him, poor pagan; where strange to say, for all the heat of his sweatings, he caught a terrible chill." (110). Not strange to say at all; it is still a common experience of those who load and unload refrigerated freight cars and truck trailers. For Queequeg it turns out that work in which cash is the exclusive motive, work that is unskilled and back-breaking, proves to be more threatening to his health than the open-air dangers of harpooneering where the joy of the chase counts for more, in his case, than cash.

It is an irony rising out of the usages of the whaling industry that Ishmael the common sailor is spared the ordeal of working in the hold alongside Queequeg. It is by deliberate choice that Ishmael avoids responsible jobs, which might in the end deprive him of human fellowship. He avoids putting his foot even on the lowest rung of the ladder of hierarchy, which leads, as Ahab knows, to the " 'desolation of solitude . . . the masoned, walled town of a Captain's exclusiveness . . . Guinea-coast slavery of solitary command" (132). Out of that isolation at the top of a hierarchy and out of forty years of assaults on whales—"the madness, the frenzy, the boiling blood and the smoking brow, with which, for a thousand lowerings old Ahab has furiously, foamingly chased his prey—more a demon than a man!"—comes an Ahab who is simultaneously champion and destroyer of humanity, champion in aspiration, destroyer in deed. He feels like "Adam, staggering beneath the piled centuries since Paradise." The burden of those centuries is the original sentence of life at hard labor and death. " 'Aye, toil we how we may, we all sleep at last on the field." It is a burden that in his way of working Ishmael tries to throw off. Ishmael would understand Ahab in order not to follow him.

Ishmael's experiences at work give him occasions to express fraternal feeling toward other workers. His solidarity with others, particularly with Queequeg, and his curiosity and playfulness at work help Ishmael assert his humanity and so help him free himself from the sway of Ahab. Because he can turn a job into an avocation, he can strengthen his integrity as a simple separate person capable of resisting a tyrant who is dehumanizing the crew. Meanwhile, that tyrant, that personification of American rugged individualism, feels commanded by a force " 'recklessly making me ready to do what in my own proper, natural heart, I durst not so much as dare."

Ishmael's forgetting of his oath of fealty to Ahab's quest is a choice of life over death, of fraternal equality over patriarchal despotism. It is no mere convenience of a plot that requires that a narrator survive a general doom. Ishmael, the unskilled intellectual worker, is the freest sailor aboard the *Pequod.* He is free of two kinds of enslavement that are typical of the crew. One kind of enslavement characterizes such maintenance workers as the carpenter, the blacksmith, and the cook. They are civilized routinists. Their work goes on day in and day out independently of the fortunes of the hunt. It is steady work because there are always repairs to be made and men to be fed. The ordinary seamen, those without special skill, are also inclined to be civilized routinists, although the rhythms of their work are determined by an irregular series of dangerous emergencies interspersed with periods of idleness of uncertain duration. To the danger that routinists in the crew might slip out of his control during their idle times, Ahab's response is to make the life of the crew as routinely busy as he can. That is why he commands them to give chase to every sperm whale sighted en route to Moby-Dick even though he has no more interest in making money. Although they are always busy, there are special reasons why the maintenance men present no problem to Ahab. The cook is a ninety-year-old black long trained to shuffle through a white man's world. The guilt-ridden alcoholic blacksmith Perth approaches work as an opportunity to do penance for the misdeeds of his life. The *Pequod*'s "singularly efficient" carpenter is characterized by Ishmael as a man of "unpersonal stolidity" with a "brain, if ever he had one," which "must early have oozed along the muscles of his fingers." He reminds Ishmael "of a common pocket-knife; but containing not only blades of various sizes, but also screw drivers, cork-screws, tweezers, awls, pens, rulers, nail-filers, countersinkers." Despite his versatility, the carpenter is a "pure manipulator" of inert materials and is himself easily available for manipulation. He is but the tool of his superiors (108). Ahab's dictatorship, in the absence of people in the crew with ability for revolutionary leadership, rests securely on alienated proletarians like the carpenter, cook, and blacksmith, but also on the unfractured precapitalist personalities of workers like Queequeg, Tashtego, and Dagoo.

Besides routinism the other enslavement Ishmael is free of is that which binds the spontaneous barbarian harpooneers. These wild aristocrats of labor, in Ishmael's view, are avid for honor and glory, not cash. They are eager volunteers in the romantic crusade against evil that Ahab has preached. To them even the gold doubloon promised to the first man to sight Moby-Dick is more a trophy than a wage. Preserving the chivalric values of precapitalist societies, they would have been content to follow Ahab in pursuit of the White Whale with never a care for profit. Ahab never had any need to manipulate them. Apart from but sharing in both the civilized and barbarian approaches to the hunt stands Ishmael, the romantic quester who goes to sea partly because he is light in pocket, short of cash, the intellectual worker ruled at last neither by the market nor by spontaneous allegiance to the goal of the commander. Yet he belongs to a crew that "seemed specially picked and packed by some infernal fatality" to give obedience to Ahab (41). What rescues him from infernal fatality? Appropriately to his view of the universe, there are elements of chance, free will, and necessity in Ishmael's escape.

It is chance that Ishmael is not on board the *Pequod* when she sinks and that Queequeg's coffin becomes his life buoy and that he is pulled out of the sea by the cruising *Rachel.* But Ishmael is not on board the *Pequod* because he replaces Ahab's harpooneer Fedallah—drowned by the whale the previous day—in Ahab's whaleboat, and Queequeg's coffin is available to him because it had been transformed into a buoy when Queequeg recovered from his nearly fatal labors stowing casks of oil in the ship's hold. At a crucial moment it turned out that the safest place to be in Moby-Dick's vicinity is in Ahab's boat and that Ishmael's survival depends in part on the death of one pagan harpooneer (Fedallah) and the near death of another (Queequeg). So much for the interpenetration of chance and necessity. There is also the element of freedom lodged in Ishmael's character and setting him off from the rest of the *Pequod*'s company. Playfully curious about the external and interior worlds, Ishmael is an American scholar, studying nature and learning to know himself while making a living. He alone of the crew is not helpless in the grasp of Ahab. Neither the civilized routinists—the officers and most of the crew—nor the spontaneous barbarians—the harpooneers—can renounce the function of tools of their commander's vengeance. To the last gasp they serve Ahab, the captain of industry presiding over an industrial despotism. They serve him even though he cares nothing for the enterprise they make their living from, cares nothing about whether they make any living at all.

At the end, with a great hole breached in the *Pequod*'s hull by the whale, Ahab gives a final command and it is obeyed. The disaster requires the display of a distress signal. While the crew sinks into the sea in a trance of submission, Tashtego, the Red Indian harpooneer, nails the red flag of disaster to the top of the mainmast and in the process blindly crucifies a screaming eagle. So it is that the last working hand, routinely doing what it is told to do, disappears.

Twined in the last tableau are two strands of the theme of work—the civilized routines of fragmented men (a good hand!) and the ferocious enthusiasm of uncivilized men for the prehistoric quest. So Melville's factory sinks, taking the national bird with it to the bottom. Shaped by his social history and his impulse to fraternity, Ishmael's unique character, expressed in his choice of work and manner of working, gives him some title to salvation, if salvation be defined as survival with an accretion of wisdom. At least it gives him title to the part of Job's messenger from that sinking factory to the world.

3.

From Drudgery to Poetry

HUMAN LABOR OF KINDS she took part in or observed is one of the resources Emily Dickinson drew on in the making of poems. She has ways of viewing work that mark her as belonging to her regional culture and ways that place her in the American economic history through which she lived. Like many others she was not at home in her culture and period. Part of her sense of homelessness is exhibited in her representation of work. How she transmits, criticizes, and transcends in poetry the view of work she inherited is the organizing question to which what follows is a response.

The social and family situation[1] from which Emily Dickinson experienced and contemplated the workaday world needs some attention before turning to her poems about work or in which work imagery is important. The Dickinsons were a provincial bourgeois family, among the powers that were in the town of Amherst, Massachusetts, during most of the nineteenth century. Emily Dickinson's grandfather, Samuel Fowler Dickinson, was a founder of Amherst College, and between 1835 and 1895 her father, Edward, and then her brother, Austin, served as treasurer of the college. Besides the college, among the many concerns of Edward Dickinson were the Massachusetts General Court, the U.S. House of Representatives, to both of which he was elected, and the Amherst and Belchertown Rail Road, of which he was president. The principal role of women in the Dickinson family was to organize the private life of a public man. Emily Dickinson, her younger sister Lavinia, and their mother Emily Norcross Dickinson filled that role, health permitting, until

Edward's death in 1874. Then the two Dickinson daughters nursed their invalid mother until she died in 1882. Four years later Emily died at age fifty-five.

Emily Dickinson was born in 1830 in the Homestead, the grand house on Main Street in Amherst built by her grandfather in 1813. When she was ten her parents and their three children moved to a smaller house. The move was occasioned by a decline in the fortunes of the Dickinson family, a result probably of the grandfather's zeal for his public causes, principally the college, to the neglect of his private affairs. While maintaining the family tradition of civic responsibility, Edward Dickinson was diligent to recoup the fortune of the family, and in 1855, after an absence of fifteen years, he triumphantly bought the Homestead back for his family. The significance of this domestic history for Emily Dickinson's poetry of work is that she opposed the return to the larger house. Among other things it meant more housework. True, there were servants, two women and a man; but it should not be supposed that the women of the family could restrict themselves to supervisory roles.

Housewifery in the United States during Emily Dickinson's formative years was changing its character. A noteworthy technical change was the adoption of the wood-burning cookstove and the abandoning of open-hearth cooking. This change is of small import for her poetry, for although Dickinson loved to cook, she makes little use of the imagery of cooking in her poems. Of greater import is the spread of the factory system and the concomittant decline of the household as a center of production. The household was becoming exclusively a center for consumption and maintenance work; for reasons other than those relating to the history of religion, the writing of a poem like Edward Taylor's "Huswifery" during Dickinson's lifetime would have been anachronistic. The Homestead, however, had some features of households of earlier centuries. Though standing on Main Street in Amherst it was a farmhouse with adjacent barn, chickens, pigs, horses, an orchard, and a field often planted to rye. The household was relatively self-sufficient, judged by the norms of an industrial society. It afforded opportunity to participate in or observe a broad range of jobs. Among her job opportunities were three she would have preferred to miss—cleaning, sewing, and tidying. But these activities above all, among the materials and of housekeeping, prove to be a source of poetic imagery for her and not those she enjoyed.

A glimpse of the daily routine of the poet as housewife is provided in *Emily Dickinson: Profile of the Poet as Cook, with Selected Recipes:*

> Even with extra help, the household's smooth functioning depended on the unceasing attention of the Dickinson women. Emily fully shared labors with her mother and sister, Lavinia, in earlier years expending herself until at "far ends of tired days," she had opportunity to turn to her books. She even exhibited a need for such work. Following an illness in 1865, she was irritated not to be able to do anything but "bang the spice for cake, and knit the soles to the stockings I knit the bodies to last June."
>
> Food preparation doubtless dominated the daily schedule. For Emily, bread and dessert-making became her special province. From this ritual service came the homely images by which she momentarily tamed nature. . . . On scraps of miscellaneous paper, even brown bags, first lines for a poem were often jotted down in pencil. If she were to "flee to her mind," she might be in mid-chore.
>
> But in the last few years of her life, when Lavinia relieved her of the more strenuous tasks, Emily admitted to keeping the "butterfly" rather than the "moth part of the house." Lavinia, convinced that Emily's role in the family was "to think," gave her time to produce her surviving work.[2]

Suggestive in this account of Dickinson as housewife and poet is the observation of her desire to do her share of the physical work of the household, her early tendency to combine doing housework and writing poetry, and her later acceptance of that division of labor in which her sister did most of the housework while she did poetry. Without insinuating any necessary causal relation, let it be noted that the bulk of her creative work was accomplished before the institution of the regime of the division of manual and mental labor in the Dickinson household.

In *Emily Dickinson and the Image of Home* Jean McClure Mudge discusses how Dickinson's life in the Homestead "put before her seemingly endless concrete materials for her poetic use." How these materials presented themselves to her partly "arose from the simple fact of being a woman. For Emily as a housekeeper, the humble article of daily use, though its upkeep annoyed and postponed the ecstatic life, still pressed on her consciousness with its symbolic potential: bones, cobwebs, cups, brooms, aprons, balls of yarn, seams, baskets, but above all, windows and doors, pantries, chambers and rooms."[3] Mudge is evidently most interested in the architectural elements in this list; here I am most interested in the nonarchitectural elements: most of them are truly in the category of "humble article of daily use" for the housekeeper. We all use windows, doors, and rooms whether we do anything to them or not; but those who work against cobwebs and with brooms, aprons, and the like are performing defining activities of the housekeeper as Dickinson experienced them.

Treated as a standard expression of the Puritan view she inherited, Edward Taylor's best-known poem, "Huswifery," can serve as a device for getting at the characteristics of Dickinson's poetry of work.

Make me, O Lord, Thy spinning wheel complete.
   Thy holy word my distaff make for me.
Make mine affections Thy swift flyers neat
   And make my soul Thy holy spool to be.
   My conversation make to be Thy reel
   And reel the yarn thereon spun of Thy wheel.

Make me Thy loom then, knit therein this twine:
   And make Thy holy spirit, Lord, wind quills:
Then weave the web Thyself. The yarn is fine.
   Thine ordinances make my fulling mills.
   Then dye the same in heavenly colors choice,
   All pinked with varnished flowers of paradise.

Then clothe therewith mine understanding, will,
   Affections, judgment, conscience, memory,
My words, and actions, that their shine may fill
   My ways with glory and Thee glorify.
   Then mine apparel shall display before Ye
   That I am clothed in holy robes for glory.

The representation of work in "Huswifery" is a way of celebrating the worker. Taylor's worker is God. When God works, humanity is the object worked on and the salvation of humanity is the goal of the work. More precisely, an individual hopes to be of that uncertain number of men and women, the elect, being worked on. The "me" prays to be a passive object of gracious divine industriousness rather than an active subject working out its own saving transformation. Yet, paradoxically, dialectically, grace works to change the self from passive raw material into a redeemed, perfected likeness of the divine subject who acts and contemplates the products of its acts—a subject united with its object, both center and circumference.

As represented by Taylor, the saving activity of God is a more arduous, heroic work than was the original creation. That was a kind of sportive, joyous play. Taylor knew "who in this bowling alley bowl'd the sun"[4] but was more appreciative of divine efforts at mastering human contrariety and inadequacy: to work at that was no child's play. Looking at the procession of metaphors in the poem, "Huswifery" is a work order or procedural manual devised by a petitioner to assist the Diety in manufacturing a new, redeemed man out of an old, fallen, natural one. It prayerfully specifies the steps by which material may be salvaged that would naturally be of no use to God or to itself, fit only to be consigned to useless perdition.

In "Huswifery" salvation is a divine cottage industry, and God is the busy housewife being asked to perform its operations. The prayerful speaker wishes to embody every substance and tool (except one) by which the housewife will make his "Holy robes for glory." The housewife's part is to supply the wool, spin the yarn and reel it, weave and full and dye the cloth, and, finally, to clothe the "understanding, will,/Affections, judgment, conscience, memory,/ . . . words, and actions" of the redeemed sinner. The housewife may then take satisfaction in contemplating her redeemed creature arrayed for glory.

The one mechanical productive force that the petitioner does not ask to become is the fulling mills. They are to be made out of the laws of God. To have failed to make this exception would have opened the petitioner to the charge that the human soul is the source of law, a transcendental heresy. Although the creator-housewife is the ultimate source of the means of production, in Marxist terms with the exception just noted, the housewife is the source of living labor and the petitioner the source of dead labor in the production of salvation. Taylor's saving God is an unalienated worker who handicrafts her product without detailed division of labor.

In some respects "Huswifery" contrasts with a typical Dickinson work poem. There is in some of her work poems the image of the creator—any creator, divine or human—as an actor who works and rests, shapes and contemplates, just as Taylor's housewife does. But her powerful worker destroys as well as crates, steals as well as saves, is Burglar as well as Banker.[5] Sometimes such antitheses are the shared aspects of a single creator for Dickinson; at other times they are embodied in contending beings. Here, for instance, is Poem 605 in which two workers are at war, one of which is a type of creativity and the other of destructiveness:

The Spider holds a Silver Ball
In unperceived Hands—
And dancing softly to Himself
His yarn of Pearl—unwinds—

He plies from Nought to Nought—
In unsubstantial Trade—
Supplants our Tapestries with His—
In half the period—

An Hour to rear supreme
His continents of Light—
Then dangle from the Housewife's Broom—
His Boundaries—forgot—

In contrast to the prayerful soul of Taylor's poem, Dickinson's spider works rather than asking to be worked on by another. He serves his own ends rather than those of another—until he is suddenly transformed from creative working subject to destroyed object of the housewife's housecleaning fury. That his work and its beauty are self-serving is suggested by the description of his web-building activity as "dancing softly to Himself." The beauty of his product is immense: his "Tapestries" are "continents of Light." Perhaps they surpass human weaving, if "supplants" carries an esthetic as well as a spatial significance in the poem. If so, they are in the tradition of the lilies of the field that surpass the raiment of Solomon in glory.

The spider's work is godlike, ex nihilo creativity: "He plies from Nought. . . . " That he plies "to Nought" as well is an acknowledgment that his creation will come to nothing. The destructive work of his nemesis, the housewife, will see to that. Until then, what he does in his hour of glory is a work of wonder. It is the manual labor of hands too tiny to see. Just as no one has seen the shaping hand of God, so human eyes can only admire the product without being able to take in the process by which the web issues from the spider's "unperceived Hands." The six words "He plies from Nought to Nought" encompass the infinite and the infinitesimal aspects of the spider's work, its origins, and result.

The activity of the spider is easy and graceful, not agonized and clumsy. To the extent that the spider worker is a nonhuman other and not a fabulous representation of the poet, his ease and grace are suggestive of the idea of work in harmony with nature, something perhaps possible beyond the boundaries of social relations, which transform work into alienated labor, degrading humanity in the process. On the other hand, one can suppose an identification of the poet with the spider like that between Whitman and his "noiseless, patient spider." Dickinson's spider belongs to the class of literal and figurative spinners of yarn that includes Taylor's divine housewife. All of them work outside the market economy, plying an "unsubstantial Trade."

In the one-sided war between the housewife and the spider, the poet is on the spider's side, but without sentimentalism. Does she also identify with the housewife in her ruthless obliteration of the boundaries of the spider's realm, her destruction of his tapestries, so that "ours" might be viewed, clear of his disfigurings? The motive of the housewife is not expressed in the poem, either to the reader or the spider. In this respect, at least, the housewife's destructive intervention into the working life of the spider has an appearance of divine arbitrariness to it.

"Bring me the sunset in a cup" (128) is the first line of a Dickinson poem, which, through a series of demands and questions, becomes a panegyric to the Worker-Creator. The form may be traced to the Voice from the Whirlwind in Job. The questions-posed—evocative of the wild and terrible beauty of the created universe—render the human audience speechless, capable only of an emotional, nonverbal response to the ineffable. A poem like Taylor's "Preface" to *God's Determinations* is an American precedent to this poem of Dickinson's when it asks "Who in this bowling alley bowl'd the sun?"

Bring me the sunset in a cup,
Reckon the morning's flagons up
And say how many Dew,
Tell me how far the morning leaps—
Tell me what time the weaver sleeps
Who spun the breadths of blue!

Write me how many notes there be
In the new Robin's ecstasy
Among astonished boughs—
How many trips the Tortoise makes—
How many cups the Bee partakes,
The Debauchee of Dews!

Also, who laid the Rainbow's piers,
Also, who leads the docile sphere
By withes of supple blue?
Whose fingers string the stalactite—
Who counts the wampum of the night
To see that none is due?

The imperatives addressed to the reader—bring, reckon, say, tell, write—are all impossible to obey. All but the first require the person addressed to respond to how many or when—to reckon up the uncountable or to reckon with the unaccountable. There are also who and whose questions put to the reader: "who laid," (evocative of opening queries in the Speech from the Whirlwind: "I will demand of thee, and answer thou me. Where wast thou when I laid the foundations of the earth? declare if thou hast understanding. Who hath laid the measure thereof if thou knowest?" (Job 38:3–5); "who leads," here descriptive of the work of the herder pulling along the obedient, haltered animals of the flock; "whose fingers string," describing the activity of the necklace-maker threading beads, "Who counts," triply suggestive of the prayerful teller of beads, the accountant making a balance (since wampum is a currency), and the numberer of the innumerable stars.

This is not a poem of unalloyed praise of Creator and creation. In the final stanza it becomes a complaint against the Creator for having given the speaker the limited perceiving powers of humanity, for having given her spiritual blindness.

Who built the little Alban House
And shut the windows down so close
My spirit can not see?

This is a bolder response to a series of unanswerable questions than Job can muster after he hears the chastening Voice from the Whirlwind. Barred from transcendent knowledge of the magnificence of the universe, flesh-and-blood humanity, it suggests, is a bad job of work, a creative bungle of the Creator. Perhaps immortality is the only remedy. The poem ends in a traditional predictive affirmation of faith in that ultimate deliverance.

Who'll let me out some gala day
With implements to fly away,
Passing Pomposity?

(128)

Or is it traditional? Like other questions posed in the poem, this last question is unanswered, perhaps because for the speaker it is unanswerable. Yet if "some gala day" does come and she is provided with wings "to fly away," the effect on her will be "Passing Pomposity," an exaltation of the self into the high perceptual and creative reaches of divinity. The means to that goal are "implements"—not natural but technical, or mechanical, means, instruments not integral to the person but tools to be grasped and used. One is reminded of Taylor's image of the saved soul's faculties clothed "in heavenly colors choice, / all pinked with varnished flowers of paradise." That too passes pomposity. For Dickinson in this poem, deliverance is from a condition in which the windows of perception are shut down close and the attainment of a condition in which those windows are wide open for mystic comprehension of Creator, creativity, and creation. It is the search for the circumference that contains all.

The Weaver God appears again in "A shady friend—for Torrid days—"(278), a poem protesting the dearth of sympathizers in the speaker's moments of anguish. Complicating Taylor's conceit, the poem affirms that the range of human characters is provided with suitable clothing by the Weaver.

A shady friend—for Torrid days—
Is easier to find—

Than one of higher temperature
For Frigid—hour of Mind—

The Vane a little to the East—
Scares Muslin souls—away—
If Broadcloth Hearts are Firmer—
Than those of Organdy—

Who is to blame? The Weaver?
Ah, the bewildering thread!
The tapestries of Paradise
So notelessly—are made!

This is Job-like, accusatory questioning. Syllogistic reasoning indicts the Weaver: if clothes make the man or woman and the Weaver weaves the cloth, the Weaver must be accountable for human character. But what is in the mind of a Weaver who makes it easier for us to find people to cool us down than to find people to warm us up? And why is salvation, the weaving of the robes of paradise, so clearly observed and represented by Taylor but so "bewildering" to Dickinson? Perhaps to ask these questions is to think about the movement from Puritanism through Transcendentalism toward Naturalism and a world in which the "Tapestries of Paradise" are "notelessly" made because one cannot observe the process, explain it, or even be sure that it is happening.

The proper relation between work and play is posed from different points of view in several poems. In Poem 231 Dickinson imagines God to be a strict organizer of the routines of production. Work, for God's subordinates, comes before play.

God permits industrious Angels—
Afternoons—to play—

He also sees that play does not take up too much time.

God calls home—the Angels—promptly—
At the Setting Sun

God's routinism cuts into her own time with an Angel with whom she has been playing at "Crown," a game of mystical rapture, a conferring or tossing of snowy hats or haloes, presumably.

A successful flight from temporal routine is celebrated in Poem 214, "I taste a liquor never brewed." The speaker is enjoying a Transcendental high.

Reeling—thro endless summer days—
From inns of Molten Blue

without a thought for work, she ends like a drunk draped around a lamp post

Leaning against the sun—

Diverted by this spectacle from their heavenly labors

. . . Seraphs swing their snowy hats—
And Saints—to windows run—

Mystical exhilaration and labor do not appear to mix; the one disrupts the other.

But the representation of an insect at work occasions meditation on the possibilities of a working life in which mystical exhilaration and labor do mix. The nectar-gathering of a worker bee gives the bee satisfactions the human worker is deprived of and longs for. Such an idealization of instinctive, nonhuman labor occurs in Poem 916. As she always does, in contravention of entomology, the poet makes her working insect masculine:

His feet are shod with Gauze—
His Helmet, is of Gold,
His breast, a Single Onyx
With Chrysophrase, inlaid.

His Labor is a Chant—
His Idleness—a Tune—
Oh, for a Bee's experience
Of Clovers, and of Noon!

Dickinson's equipping of the bee with the glittering accoutrements of a heroic warrior is like what Thoreau does when he invests the movement of railroad trains and his own house-building and hoeing with epic dignity. And if she does not intend some large distinction between "Chant" and "Tune," the song of the bee in labor and in idleness expresses the unity of work and leisure in unalienated animal activity, a unity absent from alienated human labor and leisure. Because *Chant* is associated with devotional rituals and also with work songs, as in sea chanty, the line "His Labor is a Chant" also links the bee to the Puritan sanctification of work, but without the condemnation of idleness, which is also part of the Puritan tradition. The mystical high of "a Bee's experience / Of Clover and of Noon" requires that idleness and labor be equally valued. Dickinson's bee escapes the confines of the tradition that uses the bee as a symbol of relentless industry.

Work as it is commonly experienced by suffering humanity is far from the exhilarating experience of clovers and noon. In moments of sober agony another kind of work is likely to come to mind and to come in handy. Poem 433 argues that, though not a successful therapy for the sufferer, keeping to the routines of life is a way of coping with anguish, a reason for performing "Life's little duties." These should be performed "precisely," so that even the least of them appears to be of "infinite" importance. This is painful labor:

> To simulate—is stinging work—
> To cover what we are
> From Science—and from Surgery—

This is work as a mask of prostration, a false sign that the person is self-possessed in going about her business. Such work protects private sorrows from a curious audience, who, if they pried into them, might offer "surgical" remedies or at least cutting remarks. In this mood the poet hungers to attain complete absorption in work. But that is impossible:

> We cannot put Ourself away
> As a complete Man
> Or Woman—When the Errand's done

When the task is done, the mask falls. The composure being simulated is being produced to protect the composure of others. " 'Twould start them" if they could see through the mask. So she works "For their sake—not for Ours," but also out of a desire to hang on to her sanity:

> Therefore—we do life's labor—
> Though life's reward—be done—
> With scrupulous exactness—
> To hold our Senses—on—

This is the emotionally unpaid labor of a person who senses herself to be close to a suicidal and murderous explosion:

But since we got a Bomb—
And held it in our Bosom—
Nay—Hold it—it is calm—

as the routine of daily work goes on. So the social function of reticence is to secure domestic tranquility; a calm is produced that reproduces itself in others. Meanwhile the bomb ticks away. But in this poem private suffering coexists with its antithesis, so the sufferer, generalizing her experience, speaks in the plural: misery needs company.

Poem 618 represents work as the desired remedy for psychological pain:

At leisure is the Soul
That gets a Staggering Blow—
The Width of Life—before it spreads
Without a thing to do—

It begs you give it Work—
But just the placing Pins—
Or humblest Patchwork—Children do—
To Help its Vacant Hands—

The poem indicates a motive for the kind of performance of undemanding, trivial work enumerated in Poem 443. Crude, childlike work serves the emotional requirements of the staggered soul.

Another poem of sewing (617) is a dramatic response to someone's threat to deprive her of the means of sewing because she is making such a bad job of it:

Don't put up my Thread and Needle—
I'll begin to Sew
When the Birds begin to whistle—
Better Stitches—so—

These were bent—my sight got crooked—
When my mind—is plain
I'll do seams—a Queen's endeavor
Would not blush to own—

Hems—too fine for Lady's tracing
To the sightless Knot—
Tucks—of dainty interspersion—

Like a dotted Dot—
Leave my Needle in the furrow—
Where I put it down—
I can make the zigzag stitches
Straight—when I am strong—

Till then—dreaming I am sewing
Fetch the seam I missed—
Closer—so I—at my sleeping—
Still surmise I stitch—

She has interrupted her work because the botched result dissatisfies her. She will sleep, not to escape the problem, but to dream up a solution to it. In the morning, "when the birds begin to whistle" and the solution is "plain," she will resume work, correcting what she had done before. In this description of fine needlework, sewing could be a metaphor for composing a poem. The poet begins with a tentative and mistaken effort, temporarily abandons the project, works at revision while asleep, and on awaking triumphantly returns to the making of the poem. If "don't put up my Thread and Needle" is read metaphorically, the person addressed is the poet herself, and the poem is a fragment of an internal dialogue between the self-confident believer in her creative powers and the inhibiting doubter. If the poem is read literally, two pieces of biographical data may have bearing on it. One is Emily Dickinson's complaint in a letter to Joseph Lyman that "our amiable mother never taught us tayloring [*sic*] and I am amused to remember those clothes, or rather apologies made up from dry goods with which she covered us in nursery times; so Vinnie is in the matter of raiment greatly necessary to me." Lavinia Dickinson grew ever more necessary to her sister as organizer of the home environment in which she thought and wrote. Then there is the circumstances that the poem was written about two years before the poet's eight-month's stay in Boston for treatment of impaired vision,[6] so "my sight got crooked" is not necessarily the utterance of an imagined persona. These two readings are not mutually exclusive; together they suggest how Dickinson renews old images from the workaday world.

Housework as steadying antidote for romantic longing is the theme of the first two quatrains of "If you were coming in the Fall" (511). They describe a tidying-up ritual of welcome for a lover, which grows less spontaneous and more methodical as the likelihood of disappointment increases:

If you were coming in the Fall,
I'd brush the summer by
With half a smile, and half a spurn,
As Housewives do, a Fly

If I could see you in a year,
I'd wind the months in balls—
And put them each in separate Drawers,
For fear the numbers fuse—

But beyond a season and a year the dimensions of time are simply too great to be responded to by spontaneous irritation or methodical busywork. After that comes an involuntary self-mutilation, the counting of time on the fingers until, from an excess of digital computing, they become detached from the hand and fall to the opposite side of the globe. This image goes far beyond the traditional housekeeperly description of drudgery: working the fingers to the bone.

If only Centuries delayed,
I'd count them on my Hand,
Subtracting, till my fingers dropped
Into Van Dieman's Land.

And if the wait is to be lifelong and if immortality is guaranteed, her response would be a spontaneous, untidy suicide.

If certain, when this life is out—
That yours and mine, should be
I'd toss it yonder, like a Rind,
And take Eternity—

That is not good housekeeping. But then only reasonable stretches of time can be dealt with in housekeeping fashion. Furthermore, uncertainty is worse than an annoying summer fly; immeasurable time is a terror.

But, now, uncertain of the length
Of this, that is between,
It goads me, like the Goblin Bee—
That will not state—its sting.

The apprehension of pain is frequently less bearable than realized pain. It is not to be brushed away "with half a smile, and half a spurn." The Goblin Bee is perhaps one of the bees of folklore that must be told of a death. The trajectory of responses to the absence of the longed-for one goes from the spontaneous brush-off of time, to the deliberate compression, sorting, and placing of the units of time, to the involuntarily self-mutilating counting of time in the most primitive manner, to deliberate self-annihilation. All these are conditional responses. What is absolute and not to be accommodated is the absence of uncertain duration. Its goading sting is in anticipation.

The images of work in Dickinson poems noticed so far have mostly been drawn from housecleaning and sewing, activities at which she drudged when she took part in them at all. Creative work, satisfying to the worker, tends to be represented in her poems by weaving spiders and nectar-gathering bees, unalienated, at one with nature. These toiling insects become figures of the artist creating and of the human being mystically exalted, losing the sense of human limitation. Once, however, in Poem 1034, a toiler in nature is mocked:

His Bill an Auger is
His Head a Cap and Frill
He laboreth at every Tree
A Worm, His utmost Goal

The woodpecker as carpenter bridges the gulf between nature and art. Implement and ornament are integral to this diligent worker who overlooks no possibility and seeks to nourish himself on what will ultimately nourish itself on him. The imagery of carpentry, in abstraction from nature, is explored in Poem 488:

Myself was formed—a Carpenter—
An unpretending time
My plane—and I, together wrought
Before a Builder came—

To measure our attainments—
Had we the Art of Boards
Sufficiently developed—He'd hire us
At Halves—

My Tools took Human—Faces—
The Bench, where we had toiled—

Against the Man—persuaded—
We—Temples build—I said—

If one takes "unpretending" here in the sense of earnest or serious, this would be a poem about her vocation of poetry, which she honors by comparing it to carpentry. She was formed for it and went to work at it before consulting a critic. Her work is a collaboration between herself and her tools ("My plane—and I, together wrought"). She does not expect much from the critic. The most that can be hoped for is that she and her plane will be judged competent enough to be hired at half wages. The critic who comes "to measure our attainments" hasn't an inkling of what is being tried. He supposes that what is going on is the production of boards. That is an undervaluing of the work. Under pressure of the obtuse criticism, her tools, her techniques, the instruments of her craft, "took Human—Faces—." They become sharers in the judgment, defenders of the enterprise. The very "bench, where we had toiled" becomes a witness to the seriousness of the effort, the exalted goal of the work. Against the critic, tools and bench persuade her, if not him, and she responds to uncomprehending criticism, "We—Temples build."

Dickinson makes a contribution to the georgic tradition in Poem 1025:

The Products of my Farm are these
Sufficient for my Own
And here and there a Benefit
Unto a Neighbor's Bin.

With Us, 'tis Harvest all the Year
For when the Frosts begin
We just reverse the Zodiac
And fetch the Acres in.

Here again work is a metaphor for the production of poetry. It is production outside the market economy, primarily for the use of the producer and secondarily as a gift for neighbors. Unlike the harvests of agriculture, hers are independent of the weather—the emotional not the meteorological weather, for when laboring in the fields of the imagination it is possible to run time backward as well as forward, arriving thus at whatever (emotional) season is desirable to the harvester.

A postharvest scene is caught and meditated on in Poem 1407. The aftermath is available to cows and possibly a bird:

A Field of Stubble, lying sere
Beneath the second Sun—
Its toils to Brindled People thrust—
Its Triumphs—to the Bin—
Accosted by a timid Bird
Irresolute of Alms—
Is often seen—but seldom felt,
On our New England Farms—

The stalks thrust to the cows and the grain to the bin, there remain but slim pickings for a bird. The bird alights in the field hesitantly as though doubtful of its right to a share in the harvest. Like the birds in Matthew 6:26 it has neither sown nor reaped nor gathered into barns. The reason it is timid and irresolute about its right to a living is that it is a New England bird and not a New Testament bird. The poem suggests that New England piety impatient of idlers asking for charity closes the eyes of most New England farmers to such a contrast. This little fable "is often seen—but seldom felt" by them. In this little sermon against the gospel of work, Dickinson does not see New Englandly but sees a shortcoming in seeing New Englandly.

Nature is not in New England or in any other place transformed by human labor. Perhaps a criterion of nature for Dickinson is that it is a place where birds may be bold, a place like that hinted at in Poem 1758:

Where every bird is bold to go
And bees abashless play,
The foreigner before he knocks
Must thrust the tears away.

And it is a place at the entrance to which the human foreigner may knock in vain while still ruled by the painful convicton that he is an alien in nature forever debarred from the pleasure of spontaneous, instinctual play.

The antithesis of idleness and industriousness as these traits are established by conventional signs is the theme of Poem 1685, in which Dickinson has fun with the Puritan work ethic and sumptuary tradition:

The butterfly obtains
But little sympathy
Though favorably mentioned
In Entomology—

Because he travels freely
And wears a proper coat
The circumspect are certain
That he is dissolute—

Had he the homely scutcheon
of modest Industry
'Twere fitter certifying
For Immortality—

The gadabout dandy shows no signs of election it would seem. Whoever hands out certificates of salvation is more likely to bestow them on the sober-suited and hardworking than on a butterfly. Toward the end of her life, when her younger sister had taken over most of the heavy household chores to give her time to think, "Emily admitted to keeping the 'butterfly' rather than the 'moth part of the house.' "[7] She did so arrayed in white, a color suited to a non-scrubber and duster and a self-certified candidate for immortality.

Absenting herself from the drudgery of housework inclines her to adopt a positive attitude toward cobwebs and dust. In Poem 1275 she returns to the praise of the spider's work, this time without specifying its beauties as she does in Poem 605:

The Spider as an Artist
Has never been employed—
Though his surpassing Merit
Is freely certified

By every Broom and Bridget
Throughout a Christian Land—
Neglected Son of Genius
I take thee by the Hand—

The spider has always been self-employed and always for the meeting of his own needs only, but he has never been employed by others to produce for the market even though his reputation for productivity is deservedly high. That reputation is reliably testified to "throughout a Christian Land" by every Irish houseworker and her instrument of destruction. There is a suggestion that the spider's reputation for productivity does not extend into pagan lands where perhaps he is not encountered so passionately and dealt with so relentlessly as the enemy of good housekeeping. A cataclysmic change in New England culture would have to occur before solidarity with the spider became a normal part of it. "Neglected" seems to be the wrong word to describe the cultural attitudes toward the spider this poem protests. A neglected spider would stand a good chance of surviving the frenzies of a New England housecleaning campaign.

As for dust, it is easily disposed of in Poem 1273 by being made into metaphor:

That sacred Closet when you sweep—
Entitled "Memory"— Select a reverential Broom—
And do it silently.

'Twill be a labor of surprise—
Besides Identity
Of other Interlocutors
A probability—

August the Dust of that Domain—
Unchallenged—let it lie—
You cannot supersede itself
But it can silence you—

Cleaning up such dust with an arrogant broom is bound to choke the incautious sweeper. There may be lethal surprises in such a labor. Better to proceed with "a reverential Broom" and a closed mouth; better yet to leave this imposing, accumulating, obscuring dust "unchallenged." The terrors of a too clear memory may thus be warded off.

In a laughing mood Dickinson uses the housecleaning metaphor in Poem 219, an apostrophe to a sunset personified as housewife:

She sweeps with many colored Brooms—
And leaves the Shreds behind—
Oh Housewife in the Evening West—
Come back, and dust the Pond!

You dropped a Purple Ravelling in—
You dropped an Amber thread—

And now you've littered all the East
With Duds of Emerald!

And still, she plies her spotted Brooms,
And still the Aprons fly,
Till Brooms fade softly into stars—
And then I come away—

Here she catches mockingly the cadences of the supervisor complaining to the housecleaner about her sloppy results: shreds of broom bristles are left lying, dusting is omitted, ravelling and thread are dropped, duds are littered, and still there is the appearance of great work in progress, as brooms continue to sweep and aprons to fly. The sunset is a lousy housewife and a splendid producer of beauty in disorder. The corrective supervisory commands are neither effective nor intended to be effective. The poet is playing at domesticating nature, at imposing good housekeeping procedures on the sunset. How far this is from the Puritan inclination to see divine housewifely order in nature may be sensed in these lines from Taylor's *God's Determinations:*

Who laced and filleted the earth so fine,
With rivers like green ribbons smaragdine?
Who made the seas its selvage, and it locks
Like a quilt ball within a silver box?[8]

Here are no loose ends or litter of any kind; all is neatly bound and stitched and boxed. What links Dickinson and Taylor is the continuing ability to see nature through the figures of housewifery. Between Taylor and Dickinson the economic content and the prestige of housekeeping had changed; so had the ways in which an unsentimental poet might represent it.

While considering the relation between Dickinson's housekeeping and her making of poems, the authors of *Profile of the Poet as Cook* observe that "in one poem, her pre-thunderstorm wind begins to "knead" the grass. Perhaps she seized this thought in the very act of preparing her own dough."[9] Perhaps she did, but she seems to have been uneasy with the figure, for in a second version she relinquished it. Here are the two versions of the opening quatrain of Poem 824:

The Wind begun to knead the Grass—
As Women do a Dough—
He flung a Hand full at the Plain—
A Hand full at the Sky—

The Wind begun to rock the Grass
With threatening Tunes and low—
He threw a Menace at the Earth—
A Menace at the Sky.

The first version (it is the first on the authority of Thomas H. Johnson) describes a wind violent enough to uproot turf and scatter it about in a dust storm. Did the poet, on reviewing these lines, feel that the simile of kneading dough is an inappropriate means of delivering the force of such a wind? Did she feel that the creativity of bread-making and the destructiveness of an uprooting wind were violently yoked together to no good poetic purpose, that the effect is to domesticate a wind whose wildness she wished to enhance? These are to me plausible conjectures.

In the second version she takes the wind out of the pantry and ensconces it in the nursery. "The Wind begun to rock the Grass." (The grass, we are reminded by Whitman, is "the produced babe of the vegetation.") To this babe the wind sings a scary lullaby "with threatening Tune and low." The force of the wind is less than in the first version. It does not uproot the grass and fling it about; it only makes menacing gestures at earth and sky. The wind is a crazy nurse, a potential infanticide. Violence is unrealized in the opening quatrain of the second version but it is in the first; even so, the ominous wind, bearer of menace, is no longer linked to the similitudes of normal, workaday housewifery.

An example of the use of kitchen imagery in a weather poem that apparently provoked no revisionary impulse in Dickinson in Poem 219 where falling snow is likened to sifting flour or sugar:

It sifts from Leaden Sieves—
It powders all the Wood.

The snow smooths and softens the entire landscapes, particularly the evidences of human labor—the road, the fence, the "stump, and Stack—and Stem" left behind by the harvesters of field and woodlot,

Then stills its Artisans—like Ghosts—
Denying they have been—

So the snow works with a light touch, achieving an impression of ease of performance, which makes what is done appear to the observer all but effortless, as indeed it is, for there is no human labor involved in its transformation of the landscape. A quiet and orderly proceeding (unlike the prethunderous wind), it compares well to a baker's deft sieving of flour.

Sometimes creative, sometimes destructive, sometimes a mystical rapture, sometimes an ineffective therapy for despair, work, in Dickinson poems that treat of it as fact and symbol, is sometimes close to what it is in Taylor's "Huswifery" and sometimes different. When a Dickinson work poem shows work as a defining trait of humanity tragically lacking in power to cure a sick soul, it may be said to continue the tradition exemplified by Edward Taylor. When one of her poems expresses a longing to fall out of the human condition and to fall—or rise—into an innocent nature beyond the distinctions of work and play, drudgery and ecstasy, the poem, whether it concerns the work of a human being or some nonhuman creature or creator, is a moment in the Transcendental negation of Puritanism.

4.

How Douglass Freed Himself

EMBEDDED IN THE *Narrative of the Life of Frederick Douglass, an American Slave* is an account of servile labor in different degrees of intensity. The variation, in the view of Douglass, is determined by the ideology and economic status of the different slavemasters in whose power he was during his twenty years as a slave. There is also in the *Narrative* a representation of the way slaves accept and reject enslavement as their conditions of enslavement alter because they pass from the control of one kind of master into the control of another kind, or as the character of a master itself undergoes transformation. The *Narrative* is a recruiting appeal for the abolitionist movement. It is addressed to a readership concerned for the stability of the nuclear family, the prestige of the Christian religion, and the inviolability of human minds and bodies from degrading and mutilating torments. It presents evidence, with the experience of Douglass as the principal example, that slavery subverts all these values. It acknowledges that the beneficiaries of slavery are themselves trapped in their own system, but it treats them as morally accountable for their crimes against enslaved humanity. In this it contrasts with *Uncle Tom's Cabin,* in which a benevolent owner is compelled to sell the most faithful of slaves to stave off ruin. The *Narrative,* as is appropriate for the utterance of the leader of a revolutionary movement, is saturated with the spirit of solidarity with the oppressed; it urges its readers to have nothing to do, actively or passively, with the perpetuation of slavery. My purpose is to see how Douglass presents and relates these topics in the *Narrative* and to focus on his understanding of the work experience of slaves.

In pursuit of wealth, slave masters try to get slaves to work as hard and long as possible, to work with as little hiding, sleeping, blundering, and soldiering as possible. Masters or their agents resort to several methods to reach this aim. The methods, both punishments and rewards, may be grouped in two categories, material and ideological. If punishments, they are whips that sting the flesh and whips that sting the conscience. If rewards, they somehow meet, or promise to meet, worldly human needs and spiritual strivings. Material methods, if successful, condition the slave objectively and ideological methods condition the slave subjectively. In life, however, subjective and objective are not fixed and impermeable categories, though the terms imply that they are. Human history is a record of subjects becoming objects and objects subjects. Studying history we catch the subject-object relationship in motion, freeze it momentarily, and then try to follow its complicated dance. I am doing this now in an effort to describe the way masters control slaves at work. The reader may have noticed that what I have said so far might apply to any system in which there is an exploiting class and an exploited class, not merely to the system based on chattel slavery in the American South until 1865. There is much in the system of chattel slavery as it functioned in the American South that was not peculiar to that society. The epithet "wage slaves," which Marx applies to workers living under normal capitalism, is more than invective and rhetorical exaggeration.

When a slave is lashed, the wielder of the whip is necessarily within earshot and eyesight, as well as arm's length of the slave. Responding submissively to scourging or the threat of continued scourging, a potentially free agent becomes an alienated laboring object, more acted on than acting. But the category of labor control methods exemplified by the whip has a serious drawback from the standpoint of the security of the master class and its continued expropriation of the products of servile labor. The drawback of the whip or any other method of labor control external to the worker is that it objectifies the worker, turning the potentially free producer into a servile laborer in a way readily apparent to the worker. The interest of the master class in maintaining the productivity of the slave is best served when alienating labor is not experienced in a readily recognizable form. Things go best for the master class when the slave has his or her own internal slave driver. (And for those who wish for the emancipation of labor from any and all systems of exploitation, the worst possible social and political situation exists where the internal slave driver functions smoothly in the mind of the slave; as Thoreau observes, "It is bad to have a southern overseer, it is worse to have a northern one, but worst of all to be the slave driver of yourself.") When the internal slave driver is securely ensconced in the mind of the slave, the masters are relieved of many supervisory burdens and anxieties and can pursue the dream of becoming a leisure class without a care in the world.

What is the internal slave driver? Its name is legion. Let us call implanted automatic regulatory devices ruling ideas, values, creeds. "The ruling ideas of every epoch," say Marx and Engels, "have ever been the ideas of the ruling class." The successfully indoctrinated slave is no menace to slavery, is not class conscious, is unaware of being exploited. The successfully alienated slave feels and meets obligations owed to an invisible supervisor. The felt source of these obligations is an inherited curse that defines work as an expiatory effort, punishment rather than exploitation. If the slave feels worthy of a better lot, the internal slave driver cannot function effectively. When it does function effectively, the inherited, accursed unworthiness of the slave is felt to be inexpiable in this world. It is understood then that the slave can never work off his or her sentence as an indentured servant or convict can. The successfully indoctrinated slave, the slave with a servile mentality, does have a sense of alienation, but with him or her, discontent does not give rise to outrage and rebellion. The slave so conditioned hopes for atonement, for reconciliation with the invisible supervisor and the master who is the visible representative of that supervisor. The Christian denial of salvation through works—refined and emphasized in its Calvinist variant—could become an ideological instrument for the repression of slaves in Latin and English America and Dutch South Africa. For Christianity to serve as internal slave master, it was necessary to downplay its revolutionary, egalitarian side, the side that makes it attractive to slaves who would not be slaves. (That side of Christianity currently takes the name of liberation theology.) But even slave masters, as when they were a revolutionary class in the eighteenth century, availed themselves of the revolutionary, egalitarian side of Christianity when it met their needs. Jefferson's motto was "Rebellion to tyrants is obedience to God." The paradox of revolutionary slave masters, the grotesque discrepancy between their profession and practice, caught the attention of the brilliant old Tory Samuel Johnson during the American Revolution. "How is it," he asked, "that we hear the loudest yelps for liberty among the drivers of negroes?")[1]

Frederick Douglass in his *Narrative* offers vivid examples of external and internal labor control devices and his response to them. Among those he discusses is song as a labor-control device. Listeners not involved in the labor they are associated with think of work chants as voluntary accompaniment of strenuous labor, perhaps helpful in turning work into play, drudgery into pastime. And so they may be if the work is voluntarily engaged in. And so they still may be when work is not being performed voluntarily by an association of free producers. But Douglass shows another side of the songs of working slaves, a side he contrasts to the quiet work of free workers. Douglass characterizes slave singing as "revealing at once the highest joy and the deepest sadness." He suspects "the mere hearing of those songs would do more to impress some minds with the horrible character of slavery than reading whole volumes of philosophy of the subject could do. . . . To those songs I trace my first glimmering conception of the dehumanizing character of slavery." The exultation and depression amid drudgery conveyed in slave song is understood by Douglass only after he has freed himself. "I did not, when a slave, understand the deep meaning of those rude and apparently incoherent songs. I was myself within the circle; so that I neither saw nor heard as those without might see and hear."[2] While yet a slave in mind and body, analytical detachment and generalization are not within his intellectual grasp.

Song as a control over slaves takes place when their singing is not voluntary. Such singing might have something to do with establishing the rhythm and pace of work but in the absence of the overseer it has another function. The sound of singing rising from a field testified to the whereabouts and activity of the slaves. It was good evidence that the workers were at work—good, but not foolproof evidence.

Douglass contrasts the performance of what he assumes to be the self-motivated free workers of New Bedford, Massachusetts (where he settled and went to work right after his escape from slavery), to the performance of workers he was familiar with in the South. "Almost every body seemed to be at work, but noiselessly so, compared to what I had been accustomed to in Baltimore. There were no loud songs heard from those engaged in loading and unloading ships. I heard no deep oaths or horrid curses on the laborer. . . . Every man seemed to understand his work, and went at it with a sober, yet cheerful earnestness, which betokened the deep interest which he felt in what he was doing, as well as a sense of his own dignity as a man" (115–16). However much faith ought to be put in the suggestion that noisy, domineering foremen were not likely to be encountered in Northern industry in 1838, it should not be doubted that for Douglass the singing of workers was a sign of servitude. He saw song as the expression of the slave-as-subject to his or her intensely felt but little understood condition, but also as the response of the slave-as-object to the alienating experience of exploitative production relations. At any moment one or the other side of the polarity would dominate and characterize the singing of the oppressed.

The servile side of singing has been understood for a long time. The slave who, when commanded to sing, sings is more completely enslaved than the slave who keeps silent when commanded to sing. "Sing us one of the songs of Zion" is the command of the Babylonian enslavers in Psalm 137, and the slaves from Jerusalem who are commanded to sing hope to be struck dumb if they should be so weak as to comply. From this it should not be surmised that when the spirit of revolt was strong, so was the resolve to keep silent when commanded to sing. The spirit of revolt is not constant. Douglass offers himself as an example of the instability of the slave will to keep silent when commanded to sing. When Douglass was sixteen, he was in the hands of Covey the slave breaker. Covey was pious and conducted family worship morning and evening. "Devotions were always commenced with singing; and, as he was a very poor singer himself, the duty of raising the hymn generally came upon me. He would read his hymn, and nod at me to commence. I would at times do so; at others, I would not. My noncompliance would almost always produce much confusion. To show himself independent of me, he would start and stagger through with his hymn in a most discordant manner" (74). Between the morning and evening hymn singing and prayers in the Covey household, Douglass experienced long, hard days of habituation to servile labor (slave breaking), which he bore resignedly or resisted desperately, for like every human being he could both submit to oppression and defy it. For him, there was no fixed line between physical and ideological conditioning to slavery.

The work routines and religious indoctrination experienced by Douglass both fitted and unfitted him for life in slavery. Let me now survey those experiences and instructions and his responses to them. Among influences on Douglass's experience of work are age, locale, parentage, and the wealth and health of his owner.

Douglass was born in slavery and escaped from it in 1838 at about age twenty. Before he was seven, too young to work in the fields, he had his first experience of work. "The most I had to do was drive up the cows at the evening, keeps the fowls out of the garden, keep the front yard clean, and run errands. . . . The most of my leisure time I spent in helping Master Daniel Lloyd in finding his birds, after he had shot them" (43). The locale of this initiation was the large Lloyd plantation on the eastern shore of Chesapeake Bay, a day's sail (twenty-four hours) from Baltimore. Douglass remembers suffering more from cold and hunger than from whipping during his first child labor experience. Daniel Lloyd, son of the great slaveholder Colonel Lloyd, befriended and protected him from some of the miseries of a slave childhood.

When seven or eight, Douglass was sent to be the house slave of one of his owner's relatives in Baltimore. This change of locale was good fortune for Douglass. Why did it happen? Douglass's father was white and Douglass hints that his master may have been his father. According to him, slaves sired by their masters are frequently sent away "in the first place" because they are "a constant offense to their mistress" (23). His new masters (but not owners) in Baltimore were Hugh and Sophia Auld. Douglass says going to Baltimore "laid the foundation and opened the gateway" to his liberation (46).

Being sent to Baltimore increased Douglass's desire and possibilities for escape several ways. With respect to possibilities, Baltimore, for one thing, is closer to the Mason-Dixon line than Douglass's native Talbot County, and other things being equal, the closer to the free states was a runaway's starting point, the greater the chance of escaping. Blacks, in the second place, had greater opportunities for unsupervised movement on the streets of a bustling city than they had on a plantation. The superior living conditions of urban slaves compared with rural fed Douglass's desire for liberty.

Contrary to the opinion of mechanical materialists, a sudden change in conditions for the better does not automatically palliate the resentments of the oppressed. As with Douglass, amelioration sometimes has the opposite effect. Being removed from the plantation to Baltimore gave Douglass "a deep conviction that slavery would not always be able to hold me within its foul embrace" (47). This was probably because of the improvement he felt in his own life in Baltimore and his observation of the lives of other Baltimore slaves. "A city slave," he generalizes, "is almost a freeman, compared with a slave on the plantation. He is much better fed and clothed, and enjoys privileges altogether unknown to the slave on the plantation"(50).

Douglass's first of two stays in Baltimore lasted four years. His memories of the period are dominated by his changing relationship with his new mistress, Sophia Auld, and by his struggle for literacy, an illegal acquisition for slaves throughout the South. Douglass presents the evolution of Sophia Auld as a case study in the degeneration of a good woman who had previously had no slave. As a counterpoint to that story, he provides an account of the liberating power of literacy and its accompanying joys and agonies. The story of Sophia Auld is a story of the transition of maid to matron, worker to lady and slaveholder.

> Prior to her marriage she had been dependent upon her own industry for a living. She was by trade a weaver; and by constant application to her business, she had been in a good degree preserved from the blighting and dehumanizing effects of slavery. I was utterly astonished at her goodness. I scarcely knew how to behave towards her. She was entirely unlike any other white woman I had ever seen. I could not approach her as I had approached other white ladies. My early instructions were all out of place. The crouching servility, usually so acceptable a quality in a slave, did not answer when manifested towards her. Her favor was not gained by it; she seemed to be disturbed by it. She did not deem it impudent or unmannerly for a slave to look her in the face. (48)

She started Douglass on his ABCs but her teaching was interrupted by her husband. Hugh Auld told his wife that what she was doing was against the law and that it would ruin Douglass as a useful slave. Auld predicted that Douglass "would become unmanageable and of no value to his master" and that literacy "would make him discontented and unhappy." It would be hard to imagine a keener stimulant for the desire to learn than to prohibit teaching. Douglass recalls, "I was gladdened by the invaluable instruction . . . I had gained from my master" (49). Hugh Auld had inadvertently taught him the importance of literacy.

Sophia Auld accepted her husband's order and argument, and Douglass dates the inception of her degeneration from that moment. "The first step in her downward course was in her ceasing to instruct me" (53). She ultimately outdid her husband in her opposition to Douglass's reading. "Nothing seemed to make her more angry than to see me with a newspaper. She seemed to think that here lay the danger. I have had her rush at me with a face made all up of fury, and snatch from me a newspaper, in a manner that fully revealed her apprehension" (53). Slavery and her subordination to her husband had corrupted her. She was trapped in a system she did not understand. "In entering upon the duties of a slaveholder, she did not seem to perceive that I sustained to her the relation of a mere chattel, and for her to treat me as a human being was not only wrong, but dangerously so" (52).

Hugh Auld's prediction about the effect of reading on Douglass was fully realized. "I would at times feel that learning to read had been a curse rather than a blessing. It had given me a view of my wretched condition, without the remedy. . . . In moments of agony, I envied my fellow-slaves for their stupidity. . . . It was this everlasting thinking of my condition that tormented me" (55). But still he read at every opportunity. At about twelve he was reading *The Columbian Orator,* a collection that contains a dialogue in which a slave appeals to the conscience of his master and gains his freedom by argument. He also read in this book a speech for the civil rights of Catholics by Sheridan. He studied these two pieces thoroughly. "What I got from the dialogue was the power of truth over the conscience of even a slaveholder. What I got from Sheridan was a bold denunciation of slavery, and a powerful vindication of human rights. The reading of these documents enabled me to utter my thoughts and to meet the arguments brought forward to sustain slavery" (55).

The appeal to the conscience of the slaveholder was a principle of pacifist abolitionism, which Douglass subscribed to when his *Narrative* appeared in 1845. It was to get its most memorable expression seven years later in *Uncle Tom's Cabin,* but by that time Douglass was no longer a pacifist, having been persuaded of the possibility of using the power of the federal government against slavery. What the Sheridan speech represented to Douglass was the identity of arguments to be advanced in behalf of the victims of different oppressors. What could be said for the Irish Catholics under the English Protestant establishment could as well be said for blacks enslaved in the American South. It could be said also in behalf of women, and Douglass was a lifelong supporter of the women's movement. The sympathies of Douglass for the Irish were perhaps reinforced by a childhood conversation of his with two Irish dock workers in Baltimore. Seeing the two men unloading stone from a scow, Douglass volunteered to help. They wondered whether Douglass was slave or free and, when told, one of them said "it was a shame to hold me. They both advised me to run away to the North; that I should find friends there, and that I should be free. I pretended not to be interested in what they said, and treated them as if I did not understand them; for I feared they might be treacherous" (57). They might have been true sympathizers and, then again, they might have been provocateurs on the lookout for a reward for apprehending an escaping slave. "I nevertheless remembered their advice, and from that time I resolved to run away" (57). In this episode, Douglass reveals an impulse to reach out a helping hand to white workers at work, which is modified by a cautionary restraint in the face of cordiality ostensibly evoked by his helpfulness. The episode contrasts with his experiences with white workers in a shipyard where he worked for wages.

A quarrel between Thomas Auld, who had acquired title to Douglass through marriage to the daughter of his original master, and Thomas Auld's brother, Hugh, resulted in Douglass's removal from the household of the Baltimore Aulds and his return to St. Michael's, where Thomas and Lucretia Auld lived. The change from city to country life was terrible for Douglass. It was return to the physical deprivations, the cold and hunger experienced in his first seven years made worse by the memory of the better conditions of his life in Baltimore. "It was tenfold harder after living in Master Hugh's family, where I always had enough to eat, and of that which was good" (65). The wretchedness of Douglass's new situation was aggravated by his new master.

> Captain Auld was not a born slaveholder. He had been a poor man . . . and of all men, adopted slaveholders are the worst. He was cruel but cowardly. He commanded without firmness. In the enforcement of his rules, he was at times rigid, and at times lax. At times he spoke to his slaves with the firmness of a Napoleon and the fury of a demon; at other times, he might well be mistaken for an enquirer who had lost his way. . . . He was a slaveholder without the ability to hold slaves. He found himself incapable of managing his slaves either by force, fear or fraud. We seldom called him "master." (66–67)

Against this unmasterful master, Douglass practiced a favorite act of sabotage, "letting his horse run away, and go down to his father-in-law's farm. My reason for this kind of carelessness, or carefulness, was that I could always get something to eat there" (69). Thomas Auld knew what was happening, knew Douglass was beyond his controlling, and as a last resort rented Douglass, now sixteen, to Edward Covey the slave breaker.

Douglass spent 1833 under the tutelage of Covey. A poor farmer who rented both his land and the slaves who worked it, Covey enjoyed, according to Douglass, a reputation among local slaveholders as an efficient breaker of young slaves to the discipline of work. This reputation was a condition for Covey's prospering, for some slaveholders were willing to lend Covey their young slaves rent free for the sake of his training program, and others rented their slaves cheaply in view of the value that would later accrue to them from their broken slaves (70). Covey's farm might be called an obedience school. What was practiced there still persists in principle, though in altered form, in the "educational" institutions of hierarchical societies.

The working day on the Covey farm was longer than the traditional sunup to sundown. The slaves got up in the night to feed the horses and were usually in the fields till sundown, although at "saving fodder time, midnight often caught us in the fields binding blades" (73). The working day of Covey himself was just as long as the slaves' day, with an important difference. "Covey would be out with us at the start of the day. . . . He would spend the most of his afternoons in bed. He would then come out fresh in the evening, ready to urge us on with his words, example, and frequently the whip. Mr. Covey was one of the few slaveholders who could and did work with his hands. He was a hard working man. He knew by himself just what a man or boy could do. There was no deceiving him. His work went on in his absence almost as well as in his presence; and he had the faculty of making us feel that he was ever present with us " (73). It might be said that Covey was, as portrayed by Douglass, the external compeller of labor trying to become the internal slave driver.

Covey's method exemplifies the performance of sneaky supervisers in all exploitative working situations where the payment of piecework is impractical.

> He seldom approached the spot where we were at work openly, if he could do so secretly. He always aimed at taking us by surprise. Such was his cunning, that we used to call him, among ourselves, "the snake." When we were at work in the cornfield, he would sometimes crawl on his hands and knees to avoid detection, and all at once he would rise nearly in our midst, and scream out, "Ha, ha! Come, come! Dash on, dash on!" This being his mode of attack, it was never safe to stop a single minute. . . . He was under every tree, behind every stump, in every bush, and at every window, on the plantation. He would sometimes mount his horse, as if bound to St. Michael's, a distance of seven miles, and in half an hour afterwards you would see him coiled up in the corner of the wood-fence, watching every motion of the slaves. (73)

Here was the omnipresent invisible supervisor in the flesh.

Douglass had had no experience as a field hand before going to work on the Covey farm. He speaks of his clumsiness at the unfamiliar tasks. In the first week with Covey, he was carting a load of wood from the woods when he lost control of the oxen. "I had never driven oxen before, and of course I was very awkward" (71). The runaway oxen smashed the cart into a fence gate, destroying the gate. This accident earned Douglass a whipping from Covey. During the next six months "scarce a week passed without his whipping me. I was seldom free from a sore back. My awkwardness was almost always his excuse for whipping me" (74). The effect of exhausting toil and routine ferocious punishment on Douglass was the intended one. "I was somewhat unmanageable when I first went there, but a few months of this discipline tamed me. Mr. Covey succeeded in breaking me. I was broken in body, soul and spirit. My natural elasticity was crushed, my intellect languished, the disposition to read departed . . . and behold a man turned into a brute" (75). What leisure there was for him was no longer a time to dream and learn. "Sunday was my only leisure time. I spent this in a sort of beast-like stupor, between sleep and wake, under some large tree" (75). Servile labor was matched by servile leisure. Sometimes on his leisure day, however, he would think of killing Covey and himself. It was a passing thought; he describes himself on his leisure day as being "goaded almost to madness at one moment, and at the next reconciling myself to my wretched lot" (77).

In Douglass's account of it, his experience with Covey is a cycle of degeneration and regeneration. "You have seen how a man was made a slave; you shall see how a slave was made a man" (77). Regeneration, as described by him, is object becoming subject, victim becoming victor. At the end of his first six months of servitude to Covey, an episode transformed the relationship between master and slave. There was a final bloody beating of Douglass by the slave breaker. The occasion, as was usual with his beatings, was a work situation in which Douglass had been performing unfamiliar work. It was "one of the hottest days of the month of August. . . . About three o'clock of that day, I broke down. . . . I was seized by a violent aching in the head, attended by extreme dizziness. . . . I nerved myself up, feeling it would never do to stop work. I stood as long as I could stagger to the hopper with grain. When I could stand no longer, I fell. . . . The fan of course stopped; every one had his own work to do; and no one could do the work of the other, and have his own work go on at the same time" (77). Douglass was one of four slaves put to fanning wheat, and when Covey noticed that the sound of the fan had stopped, he kicked the prostrate Douglass and beat him with a hickory slat, opening a wound in his head. As soon as Covey turned his attention away from him, Douglass fled into the woods with the intention of going to his owner for protection. But Thomas Auld refused him sanctuary. "Master Thomas ridiculed the idea that there was any danger of Mr. Covey's killing me, and said that he knew Mr. Covey, that he was a good man, and that he would not think of taking me from him; that, should he do so, he would lose the whole year's wages" (78–79). So Douglass's escape was only a twenty-four-hour respite. The next morning he had to return to the Covey farm for the final confrontation. Fortunately for him, it was Sunday and this gave him an additional day to recover his strength. Then on Monday came the confrontation. While Douglass was feeding the horses before dawn for the day's work in the fields, Covey tackled him.

> As soon as I found out what he was up to, I gave a sudden spring, and as I did so, he holding my legs, I was brought sprawling on the stable floor. Mr. Covey seemed now to think he had me, and could do what he pleased; but at this moment—from whence came the spirit I don't know—I resolved to fight. . . . I seized Covey hard by the throat; and as I did so, I rose. He held on to me, and I to him. My resistance was so entirely unexpected that Covey seemed taken all aback. He trembled like a leaf. This gave me assurance, and I held him uneasy, causing the blood to run where I touched him with the ends of my fingers. (81–82)

This violent self-defense by Douglass should be contrasted to his passive resistance to Covey when Covey first whipped him six months earlier. Before that whipping Covey had commanded him to strip. "I made him no answer, nor did I move to strip myself" (72). The cycle of fall from man to slave and rise from slave to man is completed in these two episodes. The fall is from passive resistance into abject servility, but the rise from that nadir is to resistance by any means. Notice that he ascribes his new militant resolve to a spirit of unspecified origin. He does not adopt the Jeffersonian idea that rebellion to tyrants is obedience to God. This is interesting because he is no stranger to the habit of seeing the divine hand behind positive turns of events. About his being sent to Baltimore the first time, for instance, he writes: "I may be deemed superstitious, and even egotistical, in regarding this event as a special interposition of divine Providence in my favor. But I should be false to the earliest sentiments of my soul, if I suppressed the opinion" (47). Why, then, does he not say something similar about his resistance to Covey with its beneficial, redemptive effects? There was a tactical reason that he should not have. To ascribe violent resistance to a slave master by a slave to divine inspiration would have offended the pacifist Garrisonian abolitionists with whom Douglass was associated when he wrote his *Narrative*. More may have been involved than political tact. Intellectually, at the time he was writing, Douglass may still have believed in the possibility of ending slavery through appealing to the conscience of the slaveholders. On the plane of the abstract and the general, he could conceive of "the power of truth over the conscience of even a slaveholder" (55), but his personal experience of slaveholders and their agents gave no illustrations of this idea.

When Covey was struggling with Douglass, he called two nearby slaves to his aid in overpowering Douglass. One of them complied and was starting to tie Douglass when a kick to the midriff from Douglass put him out of action. The other refused, saying to Covey that "his master hired him out to work, and not to help whip me" (82). Behind this slave's legalistic expression of concern for his job description was the solidarity of the oppressed. Behind the other slave's willingness to tie up a rebellious slave was the equally real alienation of the oppressed. The single combat of Covey and Douglass went on for almost two hours. "Covey at length let me go, puffing and blowing at a great rate, saying that if I had not resisted, he would have not have whipped me half so much. The truth was that he had not whipped me at all" (82). For Douglass, this triumph was a transformation. "He only can understand the deep satisfaction which I experienced, who has himself repelled the bloody arm of slavery. I felt as I never felt before. It was a glorious resurrection, from the tomb of slavery, to the heaven of freedom. . . . I now resolved that, however long I might remain a slave in form, the day had passed forever when I could be a slave in fact. I did not hesitate to let it be known of me, that the white man who expected to succeed in whipping, must also succeed in killing me" (83).

Douglass remained a slave for four years after this episode and testifies that he was never whipped again. He was not sure how he was able to get away with this solo rebellion, and when he wrote about it, he could only offer this explanation: Covey could have had Douglass whipped, but "Mr. Covey enjoyed the most unbounded reputation for being a first-rate overseer and negro-breaker. . . . That reputation was at stake; and had he sent me—a boy about sixteen years old—to the public whipping post, his reputation would have been lost; so, to save his reputation, he suffered me to go unpunished" (83). For Covey, in this view, the stakes were both psychological and material. Both his machismo and his income from slave breaking would have suffered by his loss of reputation. So it was that the breaker of slaves was broken by a once broken slave who, in the process, passed from slave in form and substance to slave in form only.

Formally, Douglass passed out of the control of Covey on New Year's Day, 1834. In fact and by custom, his work for Covey ended on Christmas Day, 1833. During Christmas week the slaves had to do no more than tend the livestock. "This time we regarded as our own, by the grace of our masters; and we therefore used or abused it nearly as we pleased" (83). Douglass's account of Christmas week, 1833, is objective, a flat contrast to his account of his fight with Covey; it is about what slaves in general did with their leisure, not about what he did with his. It is also about how and why masters manage the leisure of slaves. When people are free to do as they will, character expresses itself in occupation. In Douglass's analysis of slave leisure time, he discerns three characters classes: workers, hunters, and frolicsome drinkers, athletes, dancers, and musicians. Of the first two classes he writes: "The staid, sober, thinking and industrious ones of our number would employ themselves in making corn-brooms, mats, horse-collars, and baskets; and another class of us would spend the time in hunting oppossums, hares, and coons" (84). Of what the masters thought of the hunters among their slaves Douglass has nothing to say, but he testifies that the masters disapproved of the inveterate workers among them who failed to enter into the Christmas spirit. "A slave who would work during the holidays was considered by our masters as scarcely deserving them. He was regarded as one who rejected the favor of his master" (84). Holiday workers and hunters, in the view of Douglass, were a minority of the slaves, for "by far the larger part engaged in such sports and merriments as playing ball, wrestling, running foot-races, fiddling, dancing, and drinking whiskey; and this latter mode of spending the time was by far the most agreeable to the feelings of our masters" (84). One can readily imagine the effect of this report on Northern temperance, sabbatarian, Calvinist readers, who believed it, but because Douglass was a powerful propagandist in no way affects the verity of the report. Still, it is significant that he does not flesh it out with illustrations from the Christmas week of 1833 he spent on the Covey farm. Perhaps Christmas week as observed on the farm of pious, born-again Edward Covey did not conform very closely to the generalized picture of slave holiday Douglass provides.

Whatever the facts about holiday on the Covey farm, Douglass develops a shrewd and plausible theory about the effects of holiday on slaves where drunken revelry was the norm. They are, he argues, of use to the slaveholders "in keeping down the spirit of insurrection. . . . These holidays serve as conductors, or safety-valves, to carry off the rebellious spirit of enslaved humanity" (84). There is no inconsistency in production-minded slaveholders permitting and encouraging holiday revelry. "They do not give the slaves this time because they would not like to have their work during its continuance, but because they know it would be unsafe to deprive them of it" (84–85). Holiday is a means for promoting zeal for productivity among slaves. "The slaveholders like to have their slaves spend those days in just such a manner as to make them glad of their ending and of their beginning. Their object seems to be to disgust their slaves with freedom by plunging them into the lowest depths of dissipation." Douglass instances masters who "make bets on their slaves, as to who can drink the most whiskey without getting drunk; and in this way they succeed in getting whole multitudes to drink to excess." Obscuring the line between license and liberty, they thus cheat slaves in quest of a respite from slavery "with a dose of vicious dissipation artfully labeled with the name of liberty. The most of us used to drink it down, and the result was just what might be supposed: many of us were led to think that there was little to choose between liberty and slavery. . . . So, when the holidays ended, we staggered up from the filth of our wallowing, took a long breath, and marched to the field, feeling, upon the whole, rather glad to go, from what our master had deceived us into a belief was freedom" 85). Such is Douglass's representation of saturnalia as a reinforcer of the social order, of dissipation as a goad to work. Whether Douglass himself was a Christmas reveler or whether the collective "us" in his description of the proceedings among the slaves at Christmastide simply expresses his unqualified solidarity with his enslaved brothers and sisters I have yet to learn.

On January 1, 1834, his year's rental to Covey expired, Douglass was rented to William Freeland, another slaveholder near St. Michaels. It is reasonable to surmise from this that his owner,

Thomas Auld, continued to feel unsure of his ability to manage Douglass. Perhaps Auld knew or sensed that Douglass had not been successfully broken during his year on the Covey farm. In any case, William Freeland proved to be a different kind of slaveholder from any Douglass had been familiar with. Freeland was, in most respects, the opposite of Covey. He was the decent, "educated southern gentlemen," having "some regard for honor, some reverence for justice, and some respect for humanity." He was "very passionate and fretful," but not a sneaky supervisor like Covey: "we always knew where to find him." Also unlike Covey, "he made no pretensions to, or profession of religion" (86). In short, he was the type realized in Augustine St. Clair in *Uncle Tom's Cabin,* and in Judge Driscoll in *Pudd'nhead Wilson.* Freeland, "like Mr. Covey, gave us enough to eat; but, unlike Mr. Covey, he also gave us sufficient time to take our meals. He worked us hard, but always between sunrise and sunset. He required a good deal of work to be done, but gave us good tools with which to work. His farm was large, but he employed hands enough to work it, and with ease, compared to many of his neighbors. My treatment, while in his employment, was heavenly, compared with what I experienced at the hands of Mr. Edward Covey" (88).

Douglass has two points to make about his improved working conditions at Freeland's. First, the change provides him with an occasion to launch one of his many assaults on the religiosity of slaveholders. For this reason, he praises the regime he encountered during his year at Freeland's. "I went through it without receiving a single blow. I will give Mr. Freeland the credit of being the best master I ever had, *till I became my own master*" (90). The mild nonbeliever is contrasted with the hard-driving religionist. And just in case a reader might be tempted to consider Covey an exception, Douglass generalizes on the type and then gives three other examples of it: his own master and two neighboring preachers. Of religious slaveholders, he testifies, "I have ever found them the meanest, basest, the most cruel and cowardly, of all others" (87). Of Thomas Auld, who had been converted at a Methodist camp meeting in 1832, Douglass remarks, "Prior to his conversion, he relied upon his own depravity to shield and sustain him in his savage barbarity; but after his conversion, he found religious sanction and support for his slaveholding cruelty" (67). He would ply the cowhide and quote the Proverb, "He that knoweth his master's will, and doeth it not, shall be beaten with many stripes" (68). Douglass attributes to the Reverend Daniel Weeden the maxim, "Behave well or behave ill, it is the duty of a master occasionally to whip a slave, to remind him of his master's authority." Of the Reverend Rigby Hopkins, he writes: "His chief boast was his ability to manage slaves. The peculiar feature of his government was that of whipping slaves in advance of deserving it. . . . There was not a man in the whole county, with whom the slaves who had the getting [sic] their own home, would not prefer to live, rather than with this Rev. Mr. Hopkins. And yet there was not a man any where round, who made higher professions of religion, or was more active in revivals,—more attentive to the class, love-feast, prayer and preaching meetings, or more devotional in his family,—that prayed earlier, later, louder, and longer,—than this same reverend slave-driver, Rigby Hopkins" (88).

Though its lethal invective was peculiarly Douglass's, his own portrait of the type of the religious slaveholder was typical. In his narrative of his life as a slave, Henry Bibb, for instance, recounts how title to him passed from a Kentucky preacher to a Tennessee gambler to an Indian chief on the Arkansas frontier. Each time he was sold, life got better for Bibb. The idea that the representatives of moral rectitude in slaveholding society are hardest on their slaves, while infidels and outcasts are more apt to be able to maintain a human relationship with slaves and runaways is carried on in Mark Twain's greatest novel. It celebrates the community of the poor white pariah Huckleberry Finn and the runaway Jim, whose mistress, Miss Watson, a vessel of ferocious frontier Presbyterianism, sells him down the river.

Douglass's attack on slaveholding religion made him worry about alienating the pious readers he was trying to recruit to the abolitionist movement. "I have, in several instances, spoken in such a tone and manner, respecting religion, as may possibly lead those unacquainted with my religious views to suppose me an opponent of all religion." So he appends to his *Narrative* a credo in the cadence of a curse, in which he retracts not a single word of his denunciation and moderates its tone not at all. "I love the pure, peaceable, impartial Christianity of Christ: I therefore hate the corrupt, slaveholding, women-whipping, cradle-plundering, partial and hypocritical Christianity of this land" (120). He likens the Christians of America to the scribes and Pharisees denounced by Jesus. "Dark and terrible as is this picture, I hold it to be strictly true of the overwhelming mass of professed Christians in America. They strain at a gnat, and swallow a camel. Could anything be more true of our churches? They would be shocked at the proposition of fellowshipping a *sheep*-stealer; and at the same time they hug to their communion a *man*-stealer, and brand me with being an infidel, if I find fault with them for it" (123).

The second point Douglass makes about his experiences at the Freeland farm is that improved conditions for a slave can make slavery less acceptable than it is under the harshest conditions. It was at Freeland's that he planned his first attempt to escape slavery. The attempt seems to grow easily out of the relatively liberal regime of Freeland and the Sabboth school organized by Douglass for slaves near St. Michael's. The school was for blacks wishing to learn to read and to study the Bible, and they met in the house of a free black. "They came because they wished to learn. Their minds had been starved by their cruel masters. They had been shut up in mental darkness. I taught them, because it was the delight of my soul to be doing something that looked like bettering the condition of my race. I kept up my school nearly the whole year I lived with Mr. Freeland; and, beside my Sabbath school, I devoted three evenings a week, during the winter, to teaching the slaves at home" (90). The duration and scope of Douglass's school testifies to the comparative freedom of movement and the amount of unexploited energy retained by Douglass at the end of his working day at Freeland's.

The school started with two pupils, but grew as other slaves heard about it. The school was illegal and underground. Its existence might not have bothered Freeland, but neighboring masters would not have tolerated it. "It was necessary to keep our religious masters at St. Michael's unacquainted with the fact that, instead of spending the Sabbath in wrestling, boxing, and drinking whiskey, we were trying to learn how to read the will of God; for they had much rather see us engaged in those degrading sports, than to see us behaving like intellectual, moral, and accountable beings" (89). Douglass's school promoted a sense of solidarity among the slaves, which resulted in their planning a group escape. In the *Narrative,* the account of the plan and its failure is introduced by an apostrophe to the solidarity of slaves:

> It is sometimes said that we slaves do not love and confide in one another. In answer to this assertion I can say, I never loved or confided in any people more than my fellow slaves, and especially those with whom I lived at Mr. Freeland's. I believe we would have died for each other. We never undertook to do any thing, of any importance, without mutual consultation. We never moved separately. We were one; and as much so by our tempers and dispositions, as by the mutual hardships to which we were necessarily subjected by our condition as slaves. (91)

But the solidarity of the half-dozen conspiring slaves exhorted and organized by Douglass was imperfect, for one ultimately informed against them and the group was arrested on the morning of its planned departure. Significantly, Douglass does not name the traitor. To do so would be to draw the reader's attention, if only momentarily, to the weakness of a fearful turncoat, when Douglass is determined to keep it fixed on the malevolent brutality of the oppressor. Douglass learned a lesson from the failure of the attempt, and his next—and successful—run for freedom was a solo performance.

The plan of the failed group escape had been to borrow a canoe, go northward on Chesapeake Bay from St. Michael's toward Baltimore, then walk from the head of Chesapeake Bay toward Pennsylvania. "Our reason for taking the water route was, that we were less liable to be suspected as runaways; we hoped to be regarded as fishermen" (93). Fishing, they thought, was a more legitimate activity for slaves than walking on the public roads, even at Eastertide when there was much permitted visiting among members of families living and working in different places. The idea of appearing to be engaged in some kind of work while running away from slavery also occurred to Henry Bibb. His ploy was to walk down a road with an empty halter in his hand, ostensibly looking for his master's lost horse, but intending to get permanently lost himself. As a fallback protection, Douglass had forged passes giving each escapee liberty to spend Easter weekend in Baltimore. Whether the plan would have worked was never put to the test.

Douglass, following his arrest, was held in jail for two weeks and then reclaimed by his owner, Thomas Auld, who thought of selling him into Alabama, but then reconsidered and sent him back to his brother, Hugh, in Baltimore to learn a trade. Thus began Douglass's final experience of slavery, that of a rented-out urban industrial slave. Hugh Auld rented Douglass to William Gardner, a Baltimore shipbuilder. "I was put there to learn how to caulk. It, however, proved to be a very unfavorable place for the accomplishment of this object" (99). When Douglass went to work there in the spring of 1835, the Gardner shipyard was trying to finish two man-of-war brigs, which had to launched in July, "so that when I entered all was hurry. There was no time to learn any thing. Every man had to do that which he knew how to do" (99). A result was that during his eight months at the Gardner yard, Douglass was less an apprentice caulker than he was a general helper in the shipyard, "at the beck and call of about seventy-five men. . . . At times I needed a dozen pair of hands. I was called a dozen ways in the space of a single minute. Three or four voices would strike my ears at the same moment" (99–100).

The frenzied pace of work in the shipyard and the employer's anxiety about meeting his contractural deadline for the two ships led into a racist strike by the white ship carpenters in the aftermath of which Douglass was severely injured.

> The facts in the case were these: Until a very little while after I went there, white and black ship-carpenters worked side by side, and no one seemed to see any impropriety in it. All hands seemed to be very well satisfied. Many of the black carpenters were freemen. Things seemed to be going on well. All at once, the white carpenters knocked off, and said they would not work with free colored workmen. Their reason for this, as alleged, was, that if free colored carpenters were encouraged, they would soon take the trade into their own hands, and poor white men would be thrown out of employment. They therefore felt called upon at once to put a stop to it. And, taking advantage of Mr. Gardner's necessities, they broke off, swearing they would work no longer, unless he would discharge his black carpenters. (100–101)

This episode, in which white workers showed themselves to be more afraid of free blacks than of slaves, was the beginning of Douglass's realization that the problems of black people in white America would not be at an end once they were out of slavery. It was an episode tragically representative of the tendency of American workers to prefer caste struggle to class struggle.

Douglass encountered the racism of white workers toward free blacks a second time when, newly escaped from slavery, he tried to work at his trade in New Bedford, Massachusetts. "I went in pursuit of a job of caulking; but such was the strength of prejudice against color, among the white caulkers, that they refused to work with me, and of course I could get no employment (117–18). So he learned that the struggle for justice for black humanity would have to continue. But to return to the episode of the carpenter's strike in the Gardner shipyard, although the focus of the strikers' antagonism was the free black carpenters at the outset, it widened to include all blacks in the shipyard, tradesmen and apprentices, free and slave alike. Notice that the strike demand, as reported by Douglass, is that the employer discharge all black carpenters. Nothing is said about black apprentices and helpers like Douglass, for unskilled blacks were not perceived as a threat to their jobs. In Douglass's analysis, although the demand of the strikers "did not extend to me in form, it did reach me in fact. My fellow-apprentices very soon began to feel it degrading to them to work with me. They began to put on airs, and talk about 'niggers' taking the country, saying we all ought to be killed; and being encouraged by the journeymen, they commenced to make my condition as hard as they could, by hectoring me around, and sometimes striking me" (101). The upshot was that four white apprentices jumped him. He was kicked in the eye, but then picked up a handspike and chased his tormentors. "But here the carpenters interfered, and I thought I might as well give it up. It was impossible to stand my hand against so many. All this took place in sight of not less than fifty ship-carpenters, and not one interposed a friendly word" (101). It was a battle royal, entertaining to the older white workers so long as their champions were not in jeopardy. In Douglass's telling of it, he is impelled to justify not committing revolutionary suicide, as though his honor were at stake as well as his resolution to take no violence from whites made after his fight with Covey. The audience was exhorting the apprentices, " 'Kill the damned nigger! Kill him! Kill him! He struck a white person!' I found my only chance for life was in flight. I succeeded in getting away without an additional blow, and barely so; for to strike a white man is death by Lynch law" (101).

Hugh Auld was outraged at the treatment of Douglass and at his being run out of the Gardner shipyard. His motives are not specified by Douglass, but humanity and self-interest, alternatively or jointly, may be assumed. In any event, Hugh Auld appeared to Douglass at that moment in a much better light than did his brother. "I am happy to say of him, irreligious as he was; his conduct was heavenly, compared with that of his brother Thomas under similar circumstances" (102). When Douglass had appeared at the door of Thomas Auld bloodied by Covey, born-again Thomas Auld had sent him back to Covey for more of the same treatment. What Hugh Auld did, by contrast, was to try to take legal action against the assailants and then put Douglass in another shipyard (where Auld was a foreman) after Douglass had recuperated. In the new shipyard, Douglass was an apprentice in fact as well as in name, for he had a chance to learn his trade. "I was immediately set to calking, and very soon learned the act of using my mallet and irons. In the course of one year from the time I left Mr. Gardner's, I was able to command the highest wages given to the most experienced calkers. I was now of some importance to my master. I was bringing him from six to seven dollars a week. I sometimes brought him nine dollars a week" (103). Never had his conditions of slave labor been as good as they now became. Never under slavery was he so much his own master as now. "I sought my own employment, made my own contracts, and collected the money which I earned" (103). Furthermore, his time was his own when there was no work to be had in his trade.

> During these leisure times, those old notions about freedom would steal over me again. When in Mr. Gardner's employment, I was kept in such a perpetual whirl of excitement, I could think of nothing, scarcely, but my life; and in thinking of my life, I almost forgot my liberty. I have observed this in my experience of slavery,—that whenever my condition was improved, instead of its increasing my contentment, it only increased my desire to be free, and set me to thinking of plans to gain my freedom. I have found that, in order to make a contented slave, it is necessary to make a thoughtless one. (103)

Earlier, he had learned that to make a thoughtless slave, it often sufficed to burden him or her with exhausting, stupifying labor. Now, in the leisure associated with his skill-demanding work, his mind was active, and it was agitated, not only by the dignity-conferring nature of his work, but also by the nakedness of the relations of exploitation existing between himself and his master, to whom he had to give over the whole of his wages from calking. "And why? Not because he earned it,—not because I owed it to him,—nor because he possesses the slightest shadow of a right to it; but solely because he had the power to compel me to give it up" (104).

In 1838 Douglass and Hugh Auld experimented putting their economic relations on a cash basis. The arrangement led to a final confrontation between master and slave and to Douglass's flight from slavery. Under the arrangement

> I was allowed all my time, make all contracts with those for whom I worked, and find my own employment; and, in return for this liberty, I was to pay him three dollars at the end of each week; find myself in calking tools, and in board and clothing. My board was two dollars and a half per week. This, with the wear and tear of clothing of calking tools, made my regular expenses about six dollars per week. . . . Rain or shine, work or no work, at the end of each week, the money must be forthcoming, or I must give up my privilege. This arrangement, it will be perceived, was decidedly in my master's favor. It relieved him of all need of looking after me. His money was sure. He received all the benefits of slaveholding without its evils; while I endured all the evils of a slave, and suffered the care and anxiety of a freeman. I found it a hard bargain. (108)

What Douglass got out of it was the chance, "by the most untiring perseverance and industry," to accumulate some cash to prepare for his escape.

The arrangement lasted four months and was ended by Auld after an incident that must have put some readers in mind of the persecution of the Hebrew slaves who sought three days' leave from Pharaoh to worship the Lord in the wilderness. Douglass went to a camp meeting one weekend without first paying Auld his weekly three dollars, which was due Saturday night. "I knew that Master Hugh was in no special need of the money that night. I therefore decided to go to camp meeting, and upon my return pay him the three dollars" (109). When he did so, he found Auld in a fury. Auld "said he had a great mind to give me a severe whipping. He wished to know how I dared go out of the city without asking his permission. I told him I hired my time, and while I paid him the price he asked for it, I did not know that I was bound to ask him when and where I should go" (109). Auld then ordered Douglass back under the original system of urban industrial slave labor, where Douglass was to find work for himself but bring the whole of his wages to the master. Douglass's response to being deprived of the privilege of buying his own time was to strike. "Instead of seeking work, as I had been accustomed to do previously to hiring my time, I spent the whole week without the performance of a single stroke of work. . . . Saturday night, he called upon me as usual for my week's wages. I told him I had no wages. . . . Here we were on the point of coming to blows. He raved, and swore his determination to get hold of me. . . . He did not strike me, but told me that he would find me in constant employment in the future" (109).

Now Douglass set the date for his escape, three weeks from the day of this contest, and for three weeks he feigned capitulation to his master.

> Early on Monday morning, before Master Hugh had time to make any engagement for me, I went out and got employment of Mr. Butler, at his shipyard near the drawbridge . . . thus making it unnecessary for him to seek employment for me. At the end of this week I brought him between eight and nine dollars. He seemed very well pleased, and asked why I did not do the same the week before. He little knew what my plans were. My object in working steadily was to remove any suspicion he might entertain of my intent to run away; and in this I succeeded admirably. I suppose he thought I was never better satisfied with my condition than at the very time I was planning my escape. (109–10)

The final allusion to his work experience in Douglass's *Narrative* is his mention of his first day's work in New Bedford, after his escape. "I found employment, the third day after my arrival, in stowing a sloop with a load of oil. It was new, dirty, and hard work for me; but I went at it with a glad heart and a willing hand. I was now my own master. It was a happy moment, the rapture of which can be understood only by those who have been slaves. It was the first work, the reward of which was to be entirely my own. There was no Master Hugh standing ready, the moment I earned the money, to rob me of it" (117). His vision did not penetrate the veil that so often and so effectively obscures the exploitation of labor under the wages system. Free labor seemed to him, for the moment at least, truly free. At that rapturous moment he had yet to discover that in New Bedford he was not free to work at his own trade.

5.

Working and Loafing in Whitman's U.S.A.

TWO IMAGES OF WHITMAN may help concentrate the mind on his representations of work. One is a photograph said by Whitman to have been taken when he was thirty. The other is the lithograph of Whitman at thirty-five, chosen by him to be the frontispiece of the first edition of *Leaves of Grass.* In both portraits the subject looms up from a vacant background. In both he is standing but stands on nothing, one portrait showing the body to the knees and the other to just below the knees. Both, then, are of a man independent of all physical relationships, the very man of whose existence the skeptical Emerson doubted precisely because he had no historical context for the portrait and name of Walt Whitman, which had just met his eyes in the copy of *Leaves of Grass* Whitman sent hin in 1855.[1]

These two portraits say contrary things about the man they represent. The photograph shows the prematurely white Whitman, head erect, hat off and dangling from the right hand, serene yet penetrating gaze, wearing a loosely tied cravat and a three-piece ensemble with the vest negligently buttoned by only one of its seven buttons. Casual elegance appears to be the aimed-at effect. This is Whitman the saunterer in cities, the opera-goer, the dandy. The lithograph shows a Whitman whose graying has been almost completely reversed—only a patch of white shows in the beard. The head is cocked. The hat is on and worn at a rakish tilt. The gaze is closer to the combative than to the serene, an impression strengthened by the right arm resting akimbo, knuckles on hip. The full, open-collared shirt and workman's trousers are the antithesis of dandyism. Perhaps the frontispiece view was chosen to illustrate one of the many self-identifications of "Song of Myself."

> Apart from the pulling and hauling stands what I am,
> Stands amused, complaisant, compassionating, idle, unitary,
> Looks down, is erect, or bends an arm on an impalpable
>   certain rest,
> Looking with side-curved head curious what will come next,
> Both in and out of the game and watching and wondering at it.
> (11.75–78)[2]

But perhaps these lines would describe the photograph as well as the lithograph, except for the words "looks down," which fit neither, for both portraits present an egalitarian level gaze to the viewer. So when they are viewed together realization dawns that they are but two of the many changes of garments and attitude of a versatile actor. Beneath the disguise of the quick-change artist, however, lurk some stable characteristics. He does like to stand "apart from the pulling and hauling" though within view and hearing of the hustle and bustle of daily life: "Both in and out of the game and watching and wondering at it." And he is inclined to be amused, not bored, by the flood of experience the world steeps him in; complaisant, not irritated by its provocations; compassionating, never indifferent, toward those who suffer from it; idle, not laboring, while considering it; and, finally, "unitary"—not a fragmented, alienated self but a true individiual, both simple separate person and representative of the whole human race.

Like many who worked in the rapidly expanding American economy of the years of his adolescence and young manhood, Whitman in the 1830s and 40s became a jack of several trades. At ten he was an office boy for a doctor and a lawyer. Between ten and fourteen he was learning the printing trade. In 1835, at age fifteen and sixteen, he worked as a printer. During the next fourteen years he alternated between teaching school and editing and writing for newspapers. After becoming a Free Soil Democrat, he edited the Brooklyn *Freeman* in 1849; this was his last steady newspaper job before the appearance of *Leaves of Grass.* In the interim he ran a printing office and stationery store, free-lanced, and built houses on speculation. Out of these experiences of work, in interaction with his temperament and traditional values, comes that portion of Whitman's poetry of work formed according to rules for the making of original art proposed by Emerson in "The American Scholar": first absorb and reproduce what you pick up from your life of action and contemplation in the immediate environment, then use the direct responses of others to their experience, and, last, be influenced by the past, by tradition.

One of the first poems of work in *Leaves of Grass,* as finally organized by Whitman, is "I Hear America Singing." First published in the third edition of *Leaves* (1860), it is a programmatic poem, saturated with optimism about work in America and the responses of workers to it, and likely to be received with skepticism by readers familiar with the moods of people entering, toiling in, or quitting American factories, shops, offices, and fields.

I hear America singing, the varied carols I hear,
Those of mechanics, each one singing his as it should be blithe
    and strong,
The carpenter singing his as he measures his plank or beam,
The mason singing his as he makes ready for work, or leaves
    off work,
The boatman singing what belongs to him in his boat, the
    deckhand singing on the steamboat deck,
The shoemaker singing as he sits on his bench, the hatter
    singing as he stands,
The wood-cutter's song, the ploughboy's on his way in the
    morning, or at noon intermission or at sundown,
The delicious singing of the mother, or of the young wife at
    work, or of the girl sewing or washing,
Each singing what belongs to him or her and to none else,
The day what belongs to the day—at night the party of young
    fellows, robust, friendly,
Singing with open mouths their strong melodious songs.

It would be difficult to show that this poem meets the specifications of "The American Scholar" for the creation of original art. "I Hear America Singing" might be contrasted to the poem in which Emily Dickinson longs for a condition of unalienated work, which seems to be beyond human reach:

His labor is a Chant—
His Idleness—a Tune—

Oh, for a Bee's experience
Of Clovers, and of Noon![3]

It might even be charged against Whitman that he has written a carol in the genre of Walt Disney's aria for the Seven Dwarfs ("We Whistle While We Work"), except for one thing: what Whitman hears is "each singing what belongs to him or her and to none else." What he hears in his inner ear are not the chanties and sorrow songs of the wage and chattel slaves of 1860 but—and this is what I mean when I call the poem programmatic—songs expressive of the free development of each worker. These are the songs of unalienated workers in a classless utopia. (It should be noticed that Whitman hears no bosses singing.) Whitman's optimism focuses his eyes on the possibilities latent—or as would doubtless have it—emergent in the "filthy Presidentiad"[4] of Fillmore, Pierce, or Buchanan, for it was during the term of one of these temporizing nonentities as the struggle over slavery grew more intense that he made this poem. Millenarian optimism softens the sense of the intolerableness of an ugly present reality. Its presence in Whitman is a reason that so little satire is to be found among his announcements and celebrations. "I Hear America Singing" might best be read as prophecy: when the product is no longer expropriated from the producers, work will normally be accompanied by celebratory song—the production of worldly and spiritual goods will go on together. Whitman in this poem strikes up for the New World not as it is but as it might and will be.

In "Song of Myself" (1855), there is far more leisure than labor.

I lean and loafe at my ease observing a spear of
summer grass.

Thus Whitman positions himself at the outset of his most stupendous poem. Assuredly he is the poet of taking it easy. But why does he add a lazy, silent *e* to *loaf* in "Song of Myself"? Is it to convert this word, of all words, into a kind of signature, as if intent on possessing the word and by that means to seize the act of loafing as well? In any case the word and the deed are useful to him. Among other uses, Whitman's loafing is for contemplating work, taking in work's sights, sounds, smells. He does not have the Puritan's fear of looking idle amid busy people. If he does occasionally represent himself as a participant in work, he makes it seem that he works more for the sake of companionship and exercise than other recompense. His representations of other workers make the reader aware of their skill and fortitude but rarely, if ever, of their product and wage. When he began to inspect and respond to the world, he says in "Beginning My Studies" (1865), "the power of motion" was one of the things that drew and kept his attention. It was part of "the first step" in his journey into knowledge of the world.

> The first step I say awed me and pleas'd me so much,
> I have hardly gone and hardly wish'd to go any farther,
> But stop and loiter all the time to sing it in ecstatic
>   songs.

Whitman's attention to elemental facts is one source of the power of his poetry; his representation of work as motion, which is beautiful to observe and exhilarating to experience, is one aspect of that attention.

In "Song of Myself" the subject, the Me-Myself of the poem, has a myriad of masks and roles and is usually not working but loafing, "apart from the pulling and hauling" and "both in and out of the game and watching and wondering at it." He is amused by the pulling and hauling, compacent about it, compassionate toward those engaged in it. How is he in the game as well as out of it? In imagination he takes part in all pursuits and travels. Turning life into art, he turns work into play, as in this harvesttime vignette:

> The big doors of the country barn stand open and ready,
> The dried grass of the harvest-time loads the slow-drawn
>   wagon,
> The clear light plays on the brown gray and green intertinged,
> The armfuls are pack'd to the sagging mow.
>
> I am there, I help, I came stretch'd atop of the load,
> I felt its soft jolts, one leg reclined on the other,
> I jump from the cross-beams and seize the clover and timothy,
> And roll head over heels and tangle my hair full of wisps.
> (11.167–74)

Notice the passive constructions that suppress the active performers of the work: "The big doors . . . stand open and ready"—who opened them? "The dried grass . . . loads the slow-drawn wagon"—who loaded it? What draws the wagon slowly? "The armfuls are pack'd"—by whom? Then, abruptly, there is activity with a visible actor, but it is spontaneous, unproductive activity. Whitman conveys this quality through an assemblage of intransitive verbs: "I am," "I help," "I came," "I jump" and "roll," "one leg reclined." In context the three transitive verbs in the passage—"felt," "seize," and "tangle"—reinforce the sense of pleasure and play pervading the whole passage. Whitman's contribution to the work of haying turns out to be a restful joyride and a tumble in the hay.

Whitman's vignette of clam-digging is similarly reticent about the details of the process:

> The boatmen and clam-diggers arose early and stopt
> for me,
> I tuck'd my trowser-ends in my boots and went and
> had a good time;
> You should have been with us that day round the
> chowder-kettle.
>
> (11.182–84)

What matters most to him is not what is to be done but the invitation to go along and the fellowship of the meal that is a result of the work. One suspects that, this time, Whitman intends to take a hand in the work of gathering clams and not merely in the meal because he prepares himself to wade through the clam beds: "I tuck'd my trowser-ends in my boots." If this time he is properly in the game, there is nothing grimy, sweaty, or bloody about the process that might make him wish to escape into leisure.

Butchering is another matter. In "Song of Myself" he communes with the butcherboy when he is not actually butchering:

> The butcher-boy puts off his killing-clothes, or sharpens
> his knife at the stall in the market,
> I loiter enjoying his repartee and his shuffle and
> break-down.
>
> (11.217–18)

The boy's work does not exhaust him, for he is lively enough during his break to joke and dance. Still Whitman does not represent him in the act of butchering. He prefers to see him preparing for work (sharpening his knife) or after work (taking off his work clothes, joking and dancing).

Though averse to watching the butcherboy hacking through flesh and bones, Whitman easily enjoys the spectacle of a group of blacksmiths at work:

> Blacksmiths with grimed and hairy chests environ the anvil,
> Each has his main-sledge, they are all out, there is a
> great heat in the fire.
>
> From the cinder-strew'd threshold I follow their movements,
> The lithe sheer of their waists plays even with their
> massive arms,
> Overhand the hammers swing, overhand so slow, overhand so
> sure,
> They do not hasten, each man hits in his place.
> (11.219–24)

There is a delight in powerful, purposeful, coordinated motion of a working group here. As the smiths swing their hammers they put their backs into the stroke, and Whitman notices that their lithe waists seem no thicker than their brawny arms. He approves of their taking their time, working slow and sure. They do not get in one another's way, though massed around the anvil: "each man hits in his place." The interest of the scene is exclusively in a process in which a democratic work group exhibits the beauty of men working. Whitman shows no interest whatsoever in the product of this process. All that we know of whatever is being made is that it requires many smiths ("they are all out") working together to make it. The vignette of the blacksmiths around the anvil exemplifies the romantic doctrine that the maker and the making is more important than what is made.

More appealing to Whitman than even the group of blacksmiths working is the lone teamster at work:

> The negro holds firmly the reins of his four horses, the
> block swags underneath on its tied-over chain,
> The negro that drives the long dray of the stone-yard,
> steady and tall he stands pois'd on one leg on the
> string-piece,
> His blue shirt exposes his ample neck and breast and
> loosens over his hip-band,

His glance is calm and commanding, he tosses the slouch
  of his hat away from his forehead,
The sun falls on his crispy hair and mustache, falls on
  the black of his polish'd and perfect limbs.

I behold the picturesque giant and love him, and I
  do not stop there,
I go with the team also.

(11.224–31)

The appeal here is of poise, the grace of stance, rather than the grace of motion as with the blacksmiths. The black teamster is in an attitude of control without effort. He "holds firmly the reins of his four horses." Standing on the narrow surface of the stringpiece, his weight on one leg, he balances himself easily. He wears a work shirt like that worn by Whitman in the portrait that is in the frontispiece of *Leaves of Grass.* He embodies will and agility with no disfiguring mark of degrading toil. In contrast to our lack of information about the work of the blacksmiths, we know exactly what work is being done here: a block of stone is being carted away from the stoneyard and is to be delivered to a building site. But, as with the representations of the blacksmiths working, the focus of attention is on the man and what he is doing. The teamster is engaged in work that looks like idleness. This and that he is going somewhere, on some road, are sources of his appeal to Whitman. Whitman goes along with the team for the ride and the companionship (as in the haying and clamming episodes), not because he is curious about where the block of stone is going or how it will be used. The relationship of the teamster episode to those centering on the butcher boy and the blacksmiths exemplifies the movement of the observer who has identified himself as being in and out of the game from a position where he is out to a position where he is in. Thus with the butcher boy he has no response to the work being done, with the blacksmiths he is the admiring observer of the work, and with the teamster admiration leads to love and the decision to go along on the job. For Whitman the prospect of progress along a road is irresistable. For him travel is never travail as it might be for John Bunyan's Christian or Arthur Miller's Willie Loman but an opportunity to take in the sights, to experience the world. In the teamster he sees a man in whom work and travel are united and whose work therefore is enlivening and an appropriate means for displaying what is admirable in humanity.

In "Song of the Exposition" (1871), written for the fortieth annual exhibition of the American Institute in New York City, Whitman raises his voice

> To exalt the present and the real,
> To teach the average man the glory of his daily walk
>   and trade,
> To sing in songs how exercise and chemical life are
>   never to be baffled,
> To manual work for each and all, to plough, hoe, dig,
> To plant and tend the tree, the berry, vegetables,
>   flowers,
> For every man to see to it that he really do something,
>   for every woman too;
> To use the hammer and the saw, (rip, or cross-cut,)
> To cultivate a turn for carpentering, plastering,
>   painting,
> To work as a tailor, tailoress, nurse, hostler, porter,
> To invent a little, something ingenious, to aid the
>   washing, cooking, cleaning,
> And to hold it no disgrace to take a hand at them themselves.
> (11.139–49)

Effacing as usual the line between the historical reality of Robber Baron America and the reality of his vision, Whitman couples, also as usual, the worker's "daily walk and trade." "Daily walk" carries the range of connotations from the literal communting to and from work through conduct and experience; "trade" retains its specificity as synonym for *manual occupation* as indicated in the list that begins with "plough" and ends with "cleaning." (There is one exception in the list, "invent.") Whitman promises poems showing how the powers and drives of human nature "are never to be baffled." His list includes agriculture, the building, garment and housekeeping trades, as well as nurse, hostler, and porter. All these trades are to be glorified (along with the daily walk). The glorification requires abandonment of sexual and caste divisions of labor. Every man and woman should know and do them all, including the household chores—"and hold it no disgrace to take a hand at them themselves." This emancipation of labor will necessarily be the task of the laborers themselves, and its completion requires consciousness in every worker that what he is or she is doing is worth doing: "for every man to see to it that he really do something, for every woman too."

For the 1881 edition of *Leaves of Grass* Whitman added a parenthetical prologue to "Song of the Exposition," which connects his musings about work in the poem with the Puritan sanctification of work:

(Ah little recks the laborer,
How near his work is holding him to God,
The loving Laborer through space and time.)

The worker working is not conscious of the immense creativity embodied in work as process and product. To be concious of that would be to exalt the worker, endowing her or him unalienably with the powers of "the loving Laborer through space and time"—or, to give the thought an atheist formulation, to enable the worker to repossess powers that in a class society have been alienated from him or her. That consciousness would enter into history as a force tranforming the hierarchical plutocracy into a commonwealth of toilers. But because that consciousness is absent from history, because "little recks the laborer," Whitman feels impelled "to teach the average man the glory of his daily walk and trade." Twenty-five years after he said it in the preface to the first edition of *Leaves of Grass* Whitman has not forgotten that "the attitude of great poets is to cheer up slaves and horrify despots."[5]

"A Song for Occupations" (1885) is really a poem for those engaged in occupations, a Whitman manifesto to the workers of the United States. Two titles he had used before settling on the present one in 1881 and two he had considered using show his sense of the audience he means to address but also some uncertainty concerning what the poem is about. They are "Poem of the Daily Work of the Workmen and Workwomen of These States" (1856), "To Workingmen" (1867), "Song of Trades and Implements," and "Chant of Mechanics" (both rejected). In announcing his theme at the outset, Whitman speaks of "the labor of engines and trades and the labor of fields" (1.2). What does this mean? There is a sense in which engines labor, but in what sense do trades and fields labor? Normally we think of the labor of those who work with, at, or on engines and at trades and in fields. Perhaps what is being expressed is an animism in Whitman's mind, which endows engines, trades, and fields with a will to cooperate with human labor. Or perhaps his phrase is merely an eliptical expression of "those who labor on engines, at trades, and in fields." In any case the phrase leaves the reader with a feeling of spooky ambiguity. Perhaps it left Whitman with the same feeling and nagged him into twenty-five years of fiddling with the title. Whatever the phrase means, Whitman finds "in the labor of engines and trades and the labor of fields . . . the developments . . . the eternal meanings"—the pattern and goal of history, probably. Such a finding calls for a manifesto:

> Workmen and Workwomen!
> Were all educations practical and ornamental well display'd
>   out of me, what would that amount to?
> Were I as the head teacher, charitable proprietor, wise
>   statesman, what would that amount to?
> Were I to you as the boss employing and paying you, would
>   that satisfy you?
>
> The learn'd, virtuous, benevolent, and the usual terms,
> A man like me and never the usual terms.
>
> (11.4–9)

A most unusual manifesto: he refuses to strike the usual bargain with this audience of setting up the hierarchy of command and subordination based on prestige or cash. Instead he is faithful to the noble creed for teachers enunciated in "Song of Myself" (11.1234–36):

> I am the teacher of athletes,
> He that by me spreads a wider breast than my own proves
>   the width of my own,
> He most honors my style who learns under it to destroy
>   the teacher.

In "A Song for Occupations" the version of this creed is:

> Neither a servant nor a master I,
> I take no sooner a large price than a small price, I will
>   have my own whoever enjoys me,
> I will be even with you and you shall be even with me

If you stand at work in a shop I stand as nigh as the nighest in
the same shop.

(11.10–13)

There follows a demand for communal love and solidarity in the range of occasions and situations of life. Such relationships are to be had beyond the market economy: the poet is indifferent to price but "will have my own whoever enjoys me," in an egalitarian community.

The poem lists an enormous catalogue of occupations (none, by the way, supervisory). This is its climax because daily work is what keeps both the participants and the observer in touch with reality, and in touch with the sources of art:

The hourly routine of your own or any man's life, the shop,
yard, store, or factory,
These shows all near you by day and night—workman!
whoever you are, your daily life!
In that and them the heft of the heavist—in that and
them far more than you estimated, (and far less also,)
In them realities for you and me, in them poems
for you and me.

(11.127–30)

It ends with a rhetorical promise impossible of fulfilment:

When the psalm sings instead of the singer,
When the script preaches instead of the preacher,
When the pulpit descends and goes instead of the carver
that carved the supporting desk,
When I can touch the body of books by night or by day,
and when they touch my body back again,
When a university course convinces like a slumbering
woman or child convince,
When minted gold in the vault smiles like the night-
watchman's daughter,
When warrantee deeds loafe in chairs opposite and are my
friendly companions,
I intend to reach them my hand, and make as much of them
as I do of men and women like you.

(11.144–51)

So the first ambiguity is resolved: engines, trades, and fields do not labor, any more than psalms sing or gold smiles.

I have suggested that Whitman in "A Song for Occupations" may for a moment at the opening of the poem take an animist attitude toward some means of production—engines, trades, and fields. The possibility that, with great ambivalence, Whitman endows nonhuman means of production with a will of their own is stronger, if not a certainty, in "Song of the Broad-Axe" (1856). It may be felt in his opening description of the ax and account of its origin and function:

Weapon, shapely, naked, wan,
Head from the mother's bowels drawn,
Wooded flesh and metal bone, limb only one and
lip only one,
Gray-blue leaf by red-heat grown, helve produced
from a little seed sown,
Resting the grass amid and upon,
To be lean'd and to lean on.

(11.1–6)

This is the ax at the beginning of its history. Whitman presents it as appearing in its aspect of instrument of warfare before becoming an instrument of production, a weapon before a tool. Whitman's ax has human characteristics, for, though many products of fine crafting may be described as shapely, the most common referent of this adjective is a well-proportioned, graceful human figure; and one does not regard nonhuman animals as being either naked or clothed, wan or ruddy. Whitman's animated ax is composed of its own distinctive kind of flesh and bone. The materials are wood and metal, and these he describes as offspring of the earth and nourished by fire or as generated from a seed. The axhead, in its original, unformed condition of iron ore, is "from the mother's bowels drawn." (By whom? It is Whitman's bent, when he wants to mystify, to hide the active laborer in the passive construction.) The helve likewise is "produced," naturally, without the application of labor as an outgrowth of its seed.

The resulting ax is inevitably less than human—deformed or incomplete, with but a single lip and a single limb. Yet it is animated and is semisimian. It is a creature produced organically, by an invisible hand, if any. That is why it may have a life of its own, independent of human will. It is a potential annihilator of humanity and it is first glimpsed lying in the grass and cushioned by the grass,

Whitman's most powerful symbol of the continuity of life. The ax cannot do its intended work in the grass. It is fit there only "to be lean'd and to lean on," in other words, to be relinquished or to be used as a supporting staff by a person standing at rest. Perhaps the lush green peaceful living frame of the ax in this first view of it emphasizes its sinister potentialities: it is at rest now but will not always be so. At rest or in action, it represents one of humankind's most frightening perils. Like any weapon or tool with the potentiality of behaving in what seems to be an animated way, it is an example of technology out of control even when harmlessly at rest. Having presented the ax as an instrument that seems not made by human hands, Whitman has to try to square that ominous and spooky vision with his faith in human progress.

His ways of doing that are to acknowledge the violent evil accomplished with the ax but then to lavish attention on its beauty and utility as an instrument of peaceful progress, and to dispel his original mystification of it by listng the succession of craftsmen involved in its manufacture and use. First the evil use of the ax and its resolution:

(Whom have you slaughter'd lately European headsman?
Whose is that blood upon you so wet and sticky?)

I see the clear sunset of the martyrs,
I see from the scaffolds the descending ghosts,
Ghosts of dead lords, uncrown'd ladies, impeach'd ministers,
rejected kings,
Rivals, traitors, poisoners, disgraced chieftains and the rest.

I see those who in any land have died for the good cause,
The seed is spare, nevertheless the crop shall never run out,
(Mind you O foreign kings, O priests, the crop shall never
run out.)

I see blood wash'd entirely away from the axe,
Both blade and helve are clean,
They spirit no more blood of European nobles, they clasp no
more the necks of queens.

I see the headsman withdraw and become useless,
I see the scaffold untrodden and mouldy, I see no longer
any axe upon it,

I see the mighty and friendly emblem of the power of my own
  race, the newest, largest race.
(11.166–83)

So the state, that special body of armed men and instrument of legal terror, withers away in Europe and the ax becomes "the mighty and friendly emblem" of the building up of a prosperous and peaceful American civilization. O that unfulfillment should follow the prophets! is the lament we must utter as we try, four generations later, to understand and preserve the faith in human possibilities that was Whitman's. It is worth preserving and it will be preserved, for if "the seed is spare, nevertheless the crop shall never run out," and there are always places on earth "where fierce men and women pour forth as the sea . . . pours its sweeping and unript waves" (1.122).

As for the beauty and utility of the ax, recall that the first thing Whitman says of it is that it is shapely. Recall also that the ax as a woodworking implement is not only a feller and splitter but also a shaper of wood. Now it happens that the *shapely* and *shaper* are formed by adding suffixes to *shape,* the unifying noun of "Song of the Broad-Axe." Thus, just after the poem's opening incantation, the ax is associated with

Strong shapes and attributes of strong shapes,
  masculine trades, sights and sounds.
(1.6)

And toward the end of the poem Whitman frequently exclaims, "The shapes arise!" The repeated exclamation announces catalogues of ax wielders and their products. For instance:

The shapes arise!
Shapes of the using of axes anyhow, and the users and
  all that neighbors them,
Cutters down of wood and haulers of it . . .
Dwellers in cabins . . .
Seal fishers, whalers, arctic seamen breaking passages
  through the ice.
The shapes arise!
Shapes of factories, arsenals, foundries, markets,
Shapes of the two-threaded railroads,

Shapes of the sleepers of bridges, vast frameworks,
girders, arches,
Shapes of the fleets of barges, tows, lake and canal-craft,
river craft,
Ship-yards and dry-docks along the Eastern and Western seas,
and in many a bay and by-place,
The live-oak kelsons, the pine planks, the spars, the
hackmatack-roots for knees,
The ships themselves on their ways, the tiers of scaffolds,
the workmen busy outside and inside,
The tools lying around, the great auger and little auger,
the adze, bolt, line, square, gouge, and bead-plane.
(11.200–203, 206–15)

Whitman's focus has shifted from the ax as weapon to the ax as tool, from the ax at rest to the ax in use, from the ax in use to the users of the ax, from the users of axes to the things made by them, and back to the users of tools at work, and finally to the tools at rest, "lying around." The ax (and later its descendants and relatives) is the indispensable agent for the shaping of all these shapes, and the wielder of the ax is the indispensable principal. In "Song of the Broad-Axe" Whitman manages to keep in view the relative importance of agent and principal, and he does so despite his love for and desire to linger over the enumeration of all woodworking tools. He does so by maintaining that the free development of each person and not the state of technology or the productivity of labor is the true criterion of the value of a civilization:

What do you think endures?
Do you think a great city endures?
Or a teeming manufacturing state? or a prepared
constitution? or the best built steamships?
Or hotels of granite and iron? or any chef d'oeuvres
of engineering, forts, armaments?
Away! these are not to be cherish'd for themselves,
They fill their hour, the dancers dance, the musicians
play for them,
The show passes, all does well enough of course,
All does very well till one flash of defiance.

A great city is that which has the greatest men
and women,

If it be a few ragged huts it is still the greatest city
in the whole world.
(11.100–109)

In "Song of the Broad-Axe" Whitman would not be satisfied with a technology that could not get beyond "a few ragged huts," and he is no fetishist of technology. His utopia, like most utopias of the nineteenth century, is relizable regardless of the level of productivity. It is where these criteria hold (among others):

Where no monuments exist to heroes but in the common
words and deeds,
Where thrift is in its place, and prudence is in its place,
Where men and women think lightly of the laws,
Where the slave ceases, and the master of the slave ceases,
Where the populace rise at once against the never-ending
audacity of elected persons . . .
Where outside authority enters always after the precedence
of inside authority . . .
Where children are taught to be laws to themselves, and to
depend on themselves . . .
Where speculations on the soul are encouraged . . .
Where women walk in public processions in the streets
the same as the men,
Where they enter the public assembly and take places
the same as the men . . .
There the great city stands.
(11.117–21, 123, 125, 127–29, 134)

At this point it is appropriate to elevate from their footnotes a remark of Professors Blodgett and Bradley, the renowned editors of Whitman: "Although Marxist critics have claimed W[alt] W[hitman,] his individualistic ideality, typically concentrated here in sections 4 and 5, is clearly rooted in Jeffersonian idealism which flourished in his early environment."[6] I think it is unprofitable to carry on a tug-of-war over Whitman. It may be that (unnamed) Marxist critics have done so, and from weak grounds. But Marx and Whitman are both heirs of the eighteenth-century Enlightenment and thus recipients of ideas that were part of Jefferson's intellectual domain. Why then should they not hold important ideas in common (as well as having important differences)? Common ideas evident to a reader of "Song of the Broad-Axe" who also remembers some classical Marxism are the goal of a society without hierarchies of class or sex and the vision of the withering away of the state (symbolized in the poem by the final withdrawal and uselessness of the headsman). An important difference is Whitman's conviction that these ends can be attained regardless of the economic and technical givens in contrast to the Marxist assertion that these givens place limits on the transformation of society. Blodgett and Bradley apparently regard individualism as a decisive differentiator between Jeffersonianism and Marxism, forgetting that the *Communist Manifesto* advocates a society in which "the free development of each is the condition for the free development of all." Some Marxists have forgotten that too, who even imagine that the later Marx forgot it. But then there are Christians without charity and free enterprisers who demand state subsidies for their enterprises. It is best to approach contradictory Whitman, who includes multitudes and enters the world absorbing everything to himself that he encouters, with one's acquisitive, recruiting, or proprietary impulse well under control.

I began this chapter by alluding to two images of Whitman, one a photograph and the other a lithograph, one of the cocky workman in his carpenter's clothes, the other of the city dandy dressed in nonchalant elegance for his promenade or the opera. There is another image of Whitman of importance for understanding the place of work (and of leisure) in his poetry, an image we can have only through his words. It is of the child going forth along the seashore. That image is fleetingly glimpsed in "There Was a Child Went Forth" (1855) and "Out of the Cradle Endlessly Rocking" (1859) and more fully seen in "A Song of Joys" (1860).

> There was a child went forth every day,
> And the first object he look'd upon, that object he became,
> And that object became part of him for the day or a
>   certain part of the day,
> Or for many years or stretching cycles of years.

The child's first experience of a body of water is not of the seacoast but of the farmyard pond with its edge mired by the farm's livestock

> And the fish suspending themselves so curiously below there,
>   and the beautiful curious liquid,

And the water-plants with their graceful flat heads, all
    became part of him.

(1.1–10)

There then pass in review flashing images of the vegetation of all seasons, an old drunkard, the schoolmistress, white boys and girls on the way to school, a black boy and girl evidently not going to school, the crowds, traffic, houses and stores of a city, a village at sunset seen at a distance across a river. The poem ends with a steady gaze at the sea from the shore:

The schooner near by sleepily dropping down the tide,
    the little boat slack-tow'd astern,
The hurrying tumbling waves, quick-broken crests, slapping,
The strata of color'd clouds, the long bar of maroon-tint
    away solitary by itself, the spread of purity
    it lies motionless in,
The horizon's edge, the flying sea-crow, the fragrance
    of salt marsh and shore mud,
These became part of that child who went forth every day,
    and who now goes forth every day.

(11.35–39)

This is the child at leisure, the student of the world, alone, unalienated from all but especially at home on the edge of the sea. In "Out of the Cradle Endlessly Rocking," a poem about the origins of his own vocation, the mature poet revisits the favorite haunt of childhood.

A man, yet by these tears a little boy again,
Throwing myself on the sand, confronting the waves,
I, chanter of pains and joys, uniter of here and hereafter,
Taking all hints to use them, but swiftly leaping beyond them,
A reminiscence sing.

(11.18–22)

In deed and memory this is a person at leisure but who is in a poem about the pains that must be taken in the generation of poetry. It is mostly a night poem; the poem of the child who went forth is mostly a daylight poem. It is a poem of agonized wrestling with experience; the other is a poem of mostly passive and serene absorption of experience. It is a poem of alienated yearning and the effort to overcome it—a problem that does not exist for the child who went forth. It is a poem in which nature labors, the whispering sea, "like some old crone rocking the cradle" (1.182), and the mockingbird, weaving its lamentation of bereavement out of its throat, "the musical shuttle" (1.2). But the nature of "There Was a Child Went Forth" does not labor; it is an entertaining, passing spectacle, about the reality of which the child can afford to speculate:

> The doubts of day-time and the doubts of night-time,
> the curious whether and how,
> Whether that which appears so is so, or is it all
> flashes and specs?
> Men and women crowding fast in the street, if they
> are not flashes and specs what are they?
> (11.28–30)

But the anguished child of "Out of the Cradle" does not speculate about the reality of his experience or the tears it compels.

In going from the two poems just discussed to "A Song of Joys," one passes from serenity and from grief soothingly assuaged to veritable joy, from solitude to community, from leisure to work, specifically to a description of what is probably the first kind of work Whitman ever enjoyed doing, harvesting clams and lobsters on Long Island Sound. What links this part of "A Song of Joys" to the previous two poems is that it is also a reminiscence of the child on the shore. It might also be regarded as an expansion of three lines in "Song of Myself":

> The boatmen and clam-diggers arose early and stopt for me,
> I tuck'd my trowser-ends in my boots and went and had a
> good time;
> You should have been with us that day round the chowder-kettle.
> (11.182–84)

Sixteen lines of "A Song of Joys" add details of the narrator's attitude toward the shore, the smell of the place, the varieties of work, the tools, playful camaraderie on and off the job, the catching and cooking of lobsters. They are the poignant recollections of a man who as a child of ten was moved against his will away from his loved shore and went to work as an office boy in Brooklyn.

> O to have been brought up on bays, lagoons, creeks,
> or along the coast,

To continue to be employ'd there all my life,
The briny and damp smell, the shore, the salt weeds
exposed at low water,
The work of fishermen, the work of the eel-fisher and
clam-fisher;
I come with my clam-rake and spade, I come with my eel-spear,
Is the tide out? I join the goup of clam-diggers on the flats,
I laugh and work with them, I joke at my work like a
mettlesome young man;
In winter I take my eel-basket and eel-spear and travel out
on foot on the ice—I have a small axe to cut holes in the ice,
Behold me well-clothed going gayly or returning in the
afternoon, my brood of tough boys accompanying me,
My brood of grown and part-grown boys, who love to be with
no one else so well as they love to be with me,
By day to work with me, and by night to sleep with me.

Another time in warm weather out in a boat, to lift the
lobster-pots where they are sunk with heavy stones,
(I know the buoys,)
O the sweetness of the Fifth-month morning upon the water
as I row just before sunrise toward the buoys,
I pull the wicker pots up slantingly, the dark green lobsters
are desperate with their claws as I take them out,
I insert wooden pegs in the joints of their pincers,
I go to all the places one after another, and then row back
to the shore,
There is a huge kettle of boiling water the lobsters shall
be boil'd till their color becomes scarlet.

(11.32–47)

The narrator in this passage has aged himself into a patriarchal guide leading "my brood of grown and part-grown boys" out to and back from the joys of primitive food-gathering and is reminiscent of Thoreau as captain of a huckleberry party. But just before that he is "like a mettlesome young man" when, the tide being out, he joins "the group of clam-diggers on the flats." Joking and laughter are inseparable from working in his experience of this group, a free association of producers engaged in a nonalienated form of work. Finally he is working alone at gathering lobsters caught in lobsterpots. He knows the job well—where all the pots are sunk and buoyed and how to deal with the claws of desperate lobsters—and he is proud of his competence at the job. He rows his harvest ashore where the lobsters are to be immediately boiled and eaten rather than taken live to the market. ("You should have been with us that day round the chowder-kettle.") The agonies of lobsters are not one of his changes of garments in "A Song of Joys."

In discussing Whitman's poetry of work it has not been my wish to contend that Whitman should be seen as primarily a poet of work. Above all, in *Leaves of Grass* Whitman celebrates leisure. He is the poet of taking things easy and of a wonderful, contemplative dilation of the senses to take in everything there is. More often than not the reader finds him accepting and enclosing what is impressed upon his senses—fallow and passive, out of the game of work. And sometimes when he is with workers he is the idling clown in the group, along for the ride, for the companionship. But his unalienated identification with other human beings has more in it than a need for company. Among much else, his stance, his behavior, his response to the world always says that a human being should not be exploitable. The child going forth to enclose and possess the world is not exploitable, and Whitman remains that child always, studying, contemplating, absorbing. Yet Whitman is in the game too, and, even more than the Puritans, he sanctifies work. The Puritans had equated work with prayer. Whitman goes them one better. In "Song of Myself" he affirms that

> Seeing, hearing, feeling, are miracles, and each part and
> tag of me is a miracle.
>
> Divine am I inside and out, and I make holy whatever
> I touch or am touch'd from,
> The scent of these arm-pits aroma finer than prayer,
> This head more than churches, bibles, and all creeds.
> (11.523–26)

The smell of the sweat he works up ascends heavenward more efficaciously than does the incense of prayer. The work that requires sweat is a validation of his divinity, for in performing it he touches and is touched by the world and makes all holy. Connected with physical work and mysteriously arising from it are the potential and actual achievements of his head; they are "more than churches, bibles, and all creeds." So work, like leisure, is a way of knowing the world, the active and not the contemplative way; or perhaps both are mutually supportive aspects of knowing, needful for the transformation of experience into art in such a book as *Leaves of Grass.* He delivers that transformation to us in "Song of the Rolling Earth" in words that are more than what peers up at us from his page:

> Were you thinking that those were words, those upright
> lines? those curves, angles, dots?
> No, those are not the words, the substantial words are
> in the ground and sea,
> They are in the air, they are in you.
>
> Were you thinking that those were the words, those
> delicious sounds out of your friends' mouths?
> No, the real words are more delicious than they.
>
> (11.2–6)

Yet he gets those words to us, or rather helps us get at them through his book.

CONCLUSION:

Of My Time in The Factory and the Theme of Work

"You may fire when you are ready, Gridley."

—Admiral George Dewey

TO ARRIVE AT a coherent impression at the end of a discussion of five original writers is a challenge to an investigator who has tried to describe what he finds in them and not simply what he wants to find. Yet there are "subjective" and "objective" ways of unifying a discourse like mine. One way requires some account of the predispositions and experience of the observer; the other requires placing the writing examined in a historical continuum of thought and writing about work. What I see and argue for in a reading of five American writers is conditioned by my personal history and by a collective history and tradition of which I am aware and of which my five writers were aware. I now offer results arrived at by each of these approaches.

If I review my experience in industrial production, it is in the hope that readers will better understand and judge what I have tried to do in this study than they would if I were to pretend to objectivity, crouching behind the facade of disinterested scholar. And if I say something about a long tradition of thinking about work and workers, it is in the belief that this too will help summarize and unify the discussion. A landscape emerges more sharply patterned when viewed from afar than from close up. My effort to absorb the experience of getting a living transmuted into literature by five writers is helped along, I trust, both by my memories of my own factory experience and by my interest in the tradition of thought about working.

I am a man of the 1930s although I was not an adult in the 1930s. The Depression slanted my outlook on American society and imbued me with the conviction that capitalism is a terminally sick system. Optimism persuaded me that a desirable alternative to capitalism is fairly easily and quickly attainable. A powerful, insurgent working class, rushing into the CIO and winning the battle for unionism in open shop America, fed my optimism. But unlike most of my fellow leftists in those days, those in and around the Communist party inspired by their vision of the Soviet Union as the holy land where the evils of capitalism are no more and fraternal harmony prevails, my optimism about the alternative to capitalism—like that of all leftists beyond the pale of the Stalinized Communist party—Trotskyists, anarchists, and most social democrats—was qualified by a sense that something was going terribly wrong in Russia.

After graduating from high school in 1940 I spent a decade in shops organized by the CIO, long enough to realize there is nothing romantic about being a semiskilled factory worker. Most of the time I put in was in the B. F. Goodrich Tire and Rubber Company plant in Akron, Ohio. I was one of perhaps thousands of radical youngsters "colonized" by left parties and sects in the nation's basic industries. We were missionaries inspired to evangelize for our versions of socialism in industry and to support left caucuses in the unions. In Akron I learned to build truck tires and became acquainted with workers of the generation that created the CIO.

While thinking over my experience in the rubber factory recently, I turned to a book I had read forty years ago while working there. It is Ruth McKenney's *Industrial Valley,* which came out in 1939 and belongs to the genre of proletarian literature. Modeled on John Dos Passos's *U.S.A.*, *Industrial Valley* chronicles the coming of industrial unionism to Akron in a pastiche of reportage and fictional narrative. I reread it to jog my memory, to see how far I might agree or disagree with McKenney's descriptions and evaluations of the industrial milieu, and to consider how far, if at all, *Industrial Valley* shares characteristics of the writing about working I have studied.

McKenny covers events in Akron for four years, culminating in the first victorious strike in a rubber factory, in 1936; my memories of the place begin half a dozen years later, when the power of the organized workers to humanize conditions in the plants was at its peak. What I know about working conditions in the period McKenney describes I got from oral tradition, from the accounts of people I worked alongside who remembered what things were like before the union. I was told, for instance, that a genial, sympathetic foreman on my shift was formerly a tyrant given to sneak attacks and abusive tantrums. In open shop times one of his duties was to check tires on cars in the company parking lot. Any worker whose car had even one tire that was not a Goodrich product got fired. The union civilized him.

Remembering such an anecdote makes me aware of the paucity of anecdotal specificity in McKenney's description of life in the factory. She delivers an outsider's generalized report on what it was like. From her a reader can learn that the rubber workers endured relentless, exhausting speed-up on the job, but the way she represents the experience shows her workers more in the guise of stereotyped objects than differentiated human subjects. They are romanticized objects, distant from the viewer. They are slow-speaking, tall, lanky, noble savages; there is never an eloquent or a short or fat one among them. There were some pretty articulate people among my work mates and they came in various sizes and degrees or mixtures of sophistication and innocence. I do not fault McKenney for failing to be entirely "inside" the experience she represents. No writer achieves that, regardless of her resources of experience and imagination. She does fall short, in my view, of Whitman's ideal of being both in and out of the game, and I wonder whether her convictions about proletarian culture contributed to that falling short.

There is a school of writing "for" and "about" workers and the work experience that, ironically, arrives at a result that may be opposite to what the writer intended. A writer who sets out to celebrate democratic, fraternal aspirations can end with covert endorsements of hierarchy and perpetual servitude. The likelihood of such an unintended result increases, it seems to me, with the influence on the writer of the idea of proletarian culture and its corollary that the working class is a folk that endures and deserves and wishes to endure. The lyric of a song by Joe Glazer illustrates this point. Glazer composed "The Mill Was Made of Marble" to be sung by textile workers when he was educational director of the textile workers union:

Conclusion

The Mill Was Made of Marble

I dreamt that I had died
And gone to my reward;
A job in heaven's textile plant,
On a golden boulevard.

Where the mill was made of marble,
The machines were made out of gold,
Where nobody ever got tired,
And nobody ever got old.

It was quiet and peaceful in heaven,
There was no clatter and boom;
You could hear the most beautiful music,
As you worked at your spindle or loom.

There was no unemployment in heaven,
We worked steady all through the year;
We always had food for the children,
We were never haunted by fear.[1]

Glazer's song responds to the question whether the working class is a folk with a drive to maintain its present class status; it answers the question affirmatively and, I think, wrongly. I can conceive of a mill owner wanting to take his property and status with him into the next world, but I cannot imagine a textile worker who would like to be a textile worker forever. Evidences of working-class thought and action from Luddite machine-breaking through Horatio Alger dreams of individual emancipation to manifestations of antihierarchical class consciousness go to show that the industrial working class since its inception has wanted to get away from itself. It does not wish to endure, does not want class continuity, cannot bear the prospect of hereditary class status, much less an eternal one. But a union officialdom, like other bureaucracies, has a yen for self-perpetuation, and this perhaps is enough explanation for including a song like "The Mill Was Made of Marble" in a union songbook. The mind of a union bureaucrat is receptive to the notion of the workers as an enduring folk and out of sympathy with the idea that the workers are an alienated class. Glazer's song unconsciously yet poignantly expresses the aspirations of officialdom, for in the land of marble mills and golden machines it is only proper that the heavenly federation of labor be housed in mansions as grand as the textile mills. Nothing, according to an old bureaucrat's witticism, is too good for the workers. A like train of thought is to be found in the Soviet bureaucracy's doctrine of proletarian art and its objective correlatives of Stalinesque wedding-cake palaces of culture and sculptures of heroic Stakhanovite workers marching into the future. Counterpose that attitude to the radical democratic spirit of Thoreau's meditation on the factory system and what it does to workers: "I cannot believe that our factory system is the best mode by which men may get clothing. The condition of the operatives is becoming every day more like that of the English."[2] Though he never was one, Thoreau views work and working here from the angle of the factory worker. What it does to the worker is his primary consideration in determining whether the factory should be celebrated or deplored. In Thoreau's eyes New England's dark Satanic mills were not made of marble, nor did he imagine celestial factories housing golden machinery. When Thoreau writes about the work experience he is both in and out of the game and closer to intuiting the condition and aspirations of factory workers than celebrators of proletarian culture are apt to be.

In *Industrial Valley* McKenney presents the Akron tire builders as a notably independent, rebellious, and highly skilled sector of the work force, I concur with two-thirds of that characterization but think that, compared with the machinists, electricians, and carpenters in the plant, the tire builders might better be classed as semiskilled. Under the agreement in force in my time in the factory, an apprentice tire builder had ninety days to learn the job. Most were able to make out, meeting the daily required quota of tires, in half the contractual period. Still, if they compared themselves to those fellow workers relegated to mind-numbing, repetitive operations on assembly lines, they may have felt more than a trace of craft pride.

To build a truck tire was to start with nothing but the materials at hand—the cylindrical rubberized fabric plies and the tread—and with a machine you could start and stop yourself (unlike an assembly line or conveyor belt); and it was to end with a complete tire ready to be shaped by an air bag and cured in the pit. Tire builders were not as alienated as workers subjected to more intense, minute degrees of division of labor. Besides, there was a danger in building a truck tire, which discouraged daydreaming on the job and encouraged lively attention to the work process.

The sense of mastering physical danger is a source of craft pride. To wedge a rubberized cylinder of fabric onto a rapidly spinning steel drum without getting your steel-tipped levering spear caught between the drum and the fabric or between successive layers of fabric was a skill it could be fatal not to master. A stuck spear could catapult from the whirling drum like a stone from a sling, with hideous consequences for anyone in its trajectory. As an apprentice I once experienced getting my spear caught by the revolving drum, having it ripped out of my hands by the machine, seeing it spin several revolutions of the drum picking up speed, and then whiz down an aisle between two rows of jitterbugs—as we called the tire-building machines, because operating one of them required the worker to perform a sort of dance resembling the wild gesticulations and kicks of the popular dance of the 1930s. Fortunately my spear in flight missed everybody on the shop floor. But my close call, the blunder of a clumsy apprentice working on a machine in the design of which not too much heed had been paid to safety, an apprentice who was perceived to have paid not enough attention to cautionary instructions, put me temporarily into the category of all unskilled blunderers, the category of anybody of whom a work mate might say, "He couldn't pour piss out of a boot with the directions printed on the heel."

Reading *Industrial Valley* brings such details to mind, but such details of the work experience of tire builders do not come readily to McKenny's mind though she was a diligent researcher and considered the tire builders principal actors in her narrative. I miss counterparts of my recollections of pain and hilarity in McKenney's portrayal of rubber workers. Among the merits of Melville and Douglass as writers about work is that the perils and absurdities they experienced on the job were part of their material. There is something more than discrepancies of talent and experience between them and an exemplar of proletarian literature like McKenney. Nineteenth-century American writers about working did not write while handicapped by an ideology that reifies workers.

Discernible in *Industrial Valley* is a discord probably inevitable when a writer tries to celebrate rank and file militancy, spontaneity, and ability for self-emancipation while praising the vanguard party. As McKenney describes the dynamic of the class struggle, the workers have a culturally implanted ability to organize their liberation and yet they need the tutelage of the Communist party to achieve the desired goal. The ability of workers to manage things for themselves results from their schooling in factory production: "Accustomed to order, to precise machinery, to a pattern of work-life in which every detail fitted and no second of time was lost through mismanagement, they set about applying this discipline to their own strike. . . . [T]he strikers brought order out of enthusiastic confusion."[3] These workers would seem to need no condescending saviors; they can free themselves. But then, as victory in the strike nears, Jim Keller, secretary of the Summit County Communist party, is brought in to speak to the strikers: "The Communist Party congratulates you! The Communist Party is proud of you!"[4] It is a kind of epiphany:

> The audience crowded around Keller. Faces worked. Men licked their lips nervously.
>
> "Forgive me if we Communists take a sort of fatherly pride in your victory. Many of you sitting in this room had your first taste of organizing to fight for your rights in the Unemployed Council. The unemployed movement in Akron was the beginning of the rubber-workers union—a sort of prophecy of this very day.[5]

So perhaps the party's pedagogy, more than the experience of the factory, prepared the workers for effective industrial action. That pedagogy continues in Keller's speech when a striker wonders aloud whether Communists and Trotskyists are simply Reds with different popes. Keller straightens him out on the difference: " 'a Trotskyite,' Keller said deliberately, 'isn't a Communist. He works for the company.' The striker, still on his feet, nodded slowly. 'Ah, I git it.' Around the storeroom men nodded slowly. 'Them sons-of-bitches,' the striker growled."[6]

The suggestion that rubber workers in Akron in 1936 could be interested in the contention between the Communist party and the Trotskyists to the point of taking sides is not McKenney's alone; it was surely the shared fantasy of the contending factions on the left at the time. I was convinced of the fantastic nature of that suggestion when in the 1940s, at the onset of the Cold War, I found myself denounced by some of my fellow tire builders as some kind of Red who, despite my vehement anti-Stalinism, should be sent back to Russia. Standing in line waiting to punch out at shift's end, I became the recipient of red-baiting taunts by men behind me; I chose not to turn around and confront them because I was not an eager candidate for martyrdom. By 1951, my last year in the factory, waiting in line at the time clock became a daily ordeal for me and doubtless for many other Reds in American factories, regardless of their sect or chapel. My persecutors, whom I forgive, belonged to the same militant Akron proletariat McKenney imagines as being swayed by Communist party anti-Trotskyist invective, the same people whose deep-seated racism and macho nationalism she overlooks; she finds no fault in those just men, and that makes her representations of their humanity less convincing than they ought to be. The tire builders I remember did not want to remain proletarians. In their minds a strong sense of union solidarity coexisted with aspirations to a life more independent than working in industry—making a go at a small business or returning to the farm. And there was the hope that if they were sentenced to the factory for life, at least their children would not be. They persuaded me that celebrations of proletarian culture are alien to the working class. When I left the rubber factory to go to a university, I was congratulated by shop mates; to them I had received a commutation of sentence.

I return to *Industrial Valley* forty years after my first reading of it with a sense of the mixture of faith, hope, not much charity, talent, sympathy with the oppressed, patronizing of the oppressed, sectarian fanaticism toward leftists beyond the Communist party's pale, which speaks through McKenney's narrator and her heroic characters. The book is an authentic memento of the dynamic, promising, doomed left of the American 1930s. It also is a reminder of how ideology can get in the way of effective writing about the work experience. My five writers were spared the need for contending with the heritage McKenney was saddled with; the theory of proletarian culture had not been invented in their time. And they had the advantage of a tradition that opened rather than closed off the theme of work for literary development. What is the tradition I have in mind? It is the ancient and slowly accumulating memory of human attitudes toward making a living.

Song, proverb, myth, and words themselves in their historically evolving meanings record the range of human responses toward work. That range has been wide, probably since preliterate times, and it certainly has since the formation of classes and castes distinguished from one another by the varying degrees and quality of labor and leisure characterizing them. The division of society into antagonistic groups of people making their living in different ways most likely coincides with the first experiences of violent oppression and exploitation. The grim myth of the beginning of civilization told in Genesis from a pastoral point of view ties together the struggle of farmers against shepherds (Cain versus Abel), the repudiation of human solidarity ("Am I my brother's keeper?"—Gen. 4:9), the alienation of the first violent and civilized man from nature ("Cursed is the ground for thy sake."—Gen. 3:17), and the foundation of a city (a task achievable by farmers but not by shepherds). How the experience of exploitation leaves its mark on language and literature may be shown from two familiar proverbs. They are "All work and no play makes Jack a dull boy" and "A man works from sun to sun, a woman's work is never done."

In these two proverbs the age and sex of workers have affected their feelings about work. "All work and no play" conveys opposition to unrelieved child labor when it asserts that depriving Jack of leisure stupefies him. "A man works from sun to sun" protests the injustice of men assigning women a social destiny of leisureless daily tedium, an endless round of tasks yielding no sense of achievement. These two proverbs voice the attitudes of children and women who feel themselves to be victims of traditional work routines; to be just, they also express the view of men who sympathize with victims of economic hierarchies of age and sex. They may run counter to the views of persons strongly imbued with the work ethic and patriarchal notions of women's work. "All play and no work makes Jack a mere toy," cautions Lydia Maria Child, an American Abolitionist novelist, who apparently found "All work and no play" to be an indulgent and sentimental proverb. But as far as is known she never devised a substitute for the proverb against the drudgery of women's work. To some degree the two proverbs continue to articulate the experience of women and children and to measure the persistence around the world of patriarchal modes of oppression.

Those who first spoke out against being deprived of child's play or against being burdened with never ending work probably recognized the source of their grievance as a familiar human being, a parent, a husband, or a brother. That is no longer so easy to do. The capitalist market obscures the oppressor who is behind the oppression. The oppressor is no longer always easy to spot; he can become a spook haunting the oppressed in the public marketplace when people have to sell their skills to make a living. The oppressed feel that capricious and mysterious bad luck has subjected them to the market. Shakespeare conveys this feeling in his Sonnet 111. There he complains that Fortune "did not better for my life provide, / Than public means which public manners breeds." If only Fortune could have endowed him with an inheritance! But Fortune did not, and the poet has to live by selling his skills, acting and writing plays for a mass audience. Living under this necessity sullies his reputation and threatens to warp his character. "Thence comes it that my name receives a brand, / And almost hence my nature is subdued / To what it works in, like a dyer's hand." To live on money from an aristocratic patron and write sonnets for the patron and his friends, the poem suggests, is more honorable and natural for the poet than to supply the market for plays and live from the receipts of the theater, for to serve the mass market damages the artist's reputation and creativity. Injury to reputation and creativitiy is compared to the physical disfigurement of the dyer, who stains his hands working at his trade. Whether Shakespeare ever thought that writing sonnets is more dignified than writing plays, his complaint about his need to sell his skills in the marketplace and the harm being subject to the market does him is a Renaissance exercise in the art of grant application, which preserves ideas about the market appropriate to capitalist society and ideas about the relation of work and character that are older than capitalism.

The Bible is a good place to look for precapitalist attitudes toward work that persist in the literatures of people with a Judeo-Christian cultural legacy; classical mythology and philosophy is another. A lyric outcry in the Song of Songs disparages work as an involuntary and degrading experience. As in Shakespeare's Sonnet 111, the speaker in the Song of Songs complains of being thrust into an undesired occupation, but unlike the speaker in the sonnet, she can identify her oppressor; it is not the impersonal market or Fortune, it is her siblings. "Look not upon me because I am black, because the sun has looked upon me," the woman of the Song urges her lover. Prompting her plea is the conventional belief that a tan gotten working out in the sun mars the beauty of her complexion. It is the brand of a field hand, a sign of servitude, just as a red neck is the badge of peonage of a tenant farmer or stained fingers the mark of a dyer whose hands are immersed in the dyeing vat. And the woman's tanned skin is a sign of punishment as well as of toil. She explains that "my mother's children were angry with me; they made me the keeper of the vineyards; but my own vineyards have I not kept" (Song of Songs, 1:6). All work and no play have dulled her complexion; her outcry is a longing for rescue from oppressive labor. It is the same wish that Shakespeare puts directly to his "dear friend" of the sonnet: "Pity me then, and wish I were renew'd." In other words, if only the patron would help him recover from his fall into commercial play writing. The complaint of the woman of the Song of Songs expresses a leisure-class ideal of beauty and a conviction that doing manual work for a living is bad for any free human being. It may even be injurious to deities. The Greeks made their chief working God, Hephaestus, a cripple limping around his forge, and Xenophon asserts that manual labor puts men out of condition for engaging in the liberal pursuits of citizens.[7]

A leisure-class ideal of beauty, while excluding tanning, staining, or other visible signs of working for a living from the category of acceptable adornments, may encourage the display of impediments to physical exertion. Examples from diverse cultures include veils, immobilizing obesity, the long locks of Cavaliers and hippies, high heels, and long fingernails. The ideal can accommodate some traits in one context, which it rejects in another. A tan, when associated with sunbathing rather than working in a vineyard, is transformed from a stigma into a charm. A stained skin, when acquired from a tattooer and not in a dyer's vat, ceases to be a sign of servitude and becomes an ornament. In general, to present the appearance of leading an easy life is to keep one's own vineyard.

Celebrators of the work ethic can find proof texts in the Bible as easily as can advocates of genteel leisure. Contrast the protest against laboring in the vineyards of the woman in the Song of Songs to the praise of an industrious woman in the Proverbs of the Old Testament. There beauty seems to be irrelevant. The ideal woman, "whose price is above rubies," is the splendid organizer of a patriarchal household who "worketh willingly with her hands . . . bringeth her food from afar . . . riseth also while it is yet night, and giveth meat to her household . . . planteth a vineyard . . . layeth her hand to the spindle . . . maketh fine linen and selleth it" (Prov.

31:13–24). It would be out of character for such a paragon of domesticity to complain about her complexion or the roughness of her hands or how vulgar it makes her feel to sell the products of her labor in the marketplace. "She worketh willingly with her hands." Whether there would be any physical work for her husband to do around the house is uncertain. Perhaps in the performance of never-done woman's work she has freed him for a life of scholarly leisure, for sitting in the gates of the city to study Scripture and render judgments, or simply freed him for lounging in his bed. There might fall from the lips of a housewife exasperated by such a division of labor another proverb: "As the door turneth upon his hinges, so doth the slothful upon his bed" (Prov. 26:14). She has gotten up and started working "while it is yet night" and he appears to her, some hours later, to be a permanent, if free-swinging, fixture on the bed.

A view of work in Proverbs transcends class, sex, and generational conflicts. It is a utopian, revolutionary view of disciplined work as a means to liberation from want and oppression. The pious reader, attending to Scripture while his busy wife attends to the household, is instructed to "go to the ant . . . consider her ways . . . which having no guide, overseer, or ruler, provideth her meat in the summer and gathereth her food in the harvest" (Prov. 6:6–8). The female ant in this vignette works rationally, with foresight rather than under the goad of immediate need. The reward is a life without taskmasters, without a slave-driving state or the whip of the market, without "guide, overseer, or ruler." This utopian anthill in which the workers are the free masters of themselves is taken by John Milton to be prophetic of a "just equality" at the messianic end of history.[8] Even if the sex of the ant is an accident of grammatical gender, the celebration of self-disciplined work as a liberating activity is intended for the correction of male sluggards, for it is the assumed male reader of Proverbs who is invited to consider the ways of the ant and see the advantages in imitating her. But when it comes to industriousness there can be too much of a good thing. Interpreting the human fall from Paradise into a world of toil and sweat, Milton, perhaps influenced by the Christian endorsement of the contemplative life, portrays Eve as more inclined to work than Adam and makes her busyness the source of much trouble.

There is a contemplative antipathy to rational, foresightful work in the Sermon on the Mount. There Jesus expresses a third biblical attitude toward work, distinct from aristocratic rejection and "bourgeois" celebration of it. It is an attack on the Proverbial celebration of work. "Take no thought for your life, what ye shall eat, or what ye shall drink; nor yet for your body, what ye shall put on," he urges his audience. Like the makers of Proverbs he offers nonhuman living things as models for human conduct, but the ant, with her timely provisioning in summer for winter nourishment, cannot serve Jesus as a model. Instead he offers impulsive birds and sedate plants, the very antitheses of industriousness. "Behold the fowls of the air; for they sow not, neither do they reap, nor gather into barns; yet your heavenly Father feedeth them. . . . Consider the lilies of the field, how they grow; they toil not, neither do they spin: And yet I say unto you, That even Solomon in all his glory was not arrayed as one of these" (Matt. 6:25–29). The Proverbs ask the sluggard to consider the ant a model of liberating industriousness, but Jesus tells his hearers to imitate undomesticated fauna and flora because they are ideal, not industrious, and because they live for the day and are not anxiously working to make provision for the morrow. Because the needs of these creatures are met without any sowing, reaping, spinning, or toiling, he advises his audience that it can be so for them too.

Thoreau, sitting on the doorsill of his cabin, enjoying his solitude in a contemplative mood, thinks his fellow townsmen would regard what he is doing as sheer idleness but that it is not idleness if judged by the standards of the birds and the flowers. Dickinson describing a bird foraging in a New England farmer's field is on the side of the bird, which has neither sown nor reaped, and not on the side of the farmer who thinks that he who has not worked should not eat. Trusting in Providence they can be improvident. "But seek ye first the kingdom of God and . . . all these things shall be added unto you" (Matt. 6:33). The Lord will provide the material wants of those called to leisure and contemplation. Industriousness is a kind of impiety, a common human folly of all prisoners of anxiety, women as well as men. Martha, the sister of Mary, who works like that jewel of a housewife in Proverbs, is rebuked by Jesus for being too busy in her kitchen to pay attention to the sacred word (Luke 10:40–42).

This contemplative tradition descends to my five writers when they find ways to turn work into play or worship, when they can adopt a stance toward this world that is "amused, compassionating, idle, unitary,"[9] and when they try to free themselves of anxiety, to find sermons to nature, to "turn and live with the animals, they are so placid and self-contained."[10]

The Sermon on the Mount and the Song of Songs open up different routes to freedom from anxiety about where the next meal is coming from and about whether one's clothing and shelter are adequate. Anxious moments are brief and few in the Song of Songs. Its world is a world of the full horn of plenty overflowing with comfortable apples, promising grapes, and aromatic spices; it is an ambience of ample, sensuous leisure. In it the possibility of deprivation is only a fleeting nightmare. The world of the Song of Songs has not heard of the Fall and the sentencing of the human race to life at hard labor. It is either prelapsarian or postmillennial. Its season is a combination of spring burgeoning and effortless autumn harvest. It is a world given over to love with little occasion for work beyond, perhaps, a little shepherding. The world of the Sermon on the Mount is very different. There only the wild things are living satisfactorily, their needs well met without toil; the human beings are trapped in the routines of anxious labor. The horn of plenty is out of reach to them, unlike the happy lovers of the Song of Songs. The Sermon on the Mount seems to recommend the asceticism of voluntary poverty as a means of escape from anxiety. To abstain from work and abandon the quest for luxurious plenty is to avoid distractions from the contemplative search for the kingdom of God. It requires the daring of faith that trusts that "all things shall be added" that are necessary to sustain life. Thoreau sees in this way when he characterizes a contemplative day on the Walden shore: "This was sheer idleness to my fellow-townsmen, no doubt; but if the birds and flowers have tried me by their standard, I should not have been found wanting."[11] But for Thoreau satisfying leisure is not to be had apart from demanding work.

Until now neither the Song of Song's sensuous nor the Sermon on the Mount's ascetic way to freedom from anxiety has been available, in practice, to most human beings. Most of the race has been denied great opportunities to do as they please, living apart from the workaday world, committed to a life of play or of pious contem-plation. Humanity for the most part has had to reckon with the probability that staying alive requires lengthy, sustained, and arduous activity. This human condition appears sometimes to be sinister and sometimes wholesome. When sinister, it may give rise to fantastic apprehensions. It may, for instance, occur to me that I have to work because I have offended some familiar power, or some mysterious, unidentified power: "my mother's children were angry with me," the woman in the Song of Songs complains. Or perhaps some faceless spook was. Forcing me to work for a living, that power demonstrates hostility toward me. "Cursed is the ground for thy sake; in sorrow shalt thou eat of it all the days of thy life" (Gen. 3:17). If something had not gone wrong, a provocation to punishing wrath committed by me or my ancestors, would I not be permitted to live at leisure and take all I need at nature's generous breast in the pastoral style of the lovers in the Song of Songs, or from the hands of servitors whose workaday life I can ignore, despise, or sentimentalize because I am far removed from it by virtue of my class status? I may personify as a taskmaster the something that commands me to work, a taskmaster who—justly or unjustly, methodically or capriciously—exacts a price from me for clinging to life. Grunting and sweating like any beast of burden—not like those idle and decorative birds and flowers Jesus alludes to!—I grudgingly pay the price. Or perhaps I hopefully pay, for there is a chance my labor may expiate my offense.

In some such manner alienated humanity has developed its imaginative response to the sinister aspect of working for a living. This ancient and continuing effort to make sense out of experience is embodied in and struggled with in the best-known and most influential of all myths, the myth of the Garden and the expulsion from the Garden.

There is, however, an agreeable as well as a sinister side to the human response to working. People do find gratification in meeting human needs. Alone or in association with other workers I make something useful that may have beauty as well as utility. As I make this use-value I discover and verify endowments, the powers and talents that help define me as a separate human being and a member of a larger human group. In excellent working conditions what I make and the making of it persuade me that I am a freely developing individual, exploring the qualities of the external world as I explore the range of my abilities. Under excellent working conditions the supernatural overseer eases off on his slave driving; the sentence on Adam of life at hard labor is lifted. In the best working conditions the work to be done is a demanding test of my abilities. I must keep my mind on what I am doing. Work then has the intensity of play where one must keep one's eye on the ball.

Hence, the human response to working is a polar unity of opposites. At one pole cluster work's fatal, penitential characteristics and at the other pole work's liberating and playful characteristics. One of these poles is upppermost in every working experience whose repulsive and attractive features are not in balance. Where one or the other pole dominates, I am either going to feel that a power beyond my control is teaching me a grimly punishing lesson while I work or I am going to feel that I am freely and playfully indulging my curiosity about and mastery over my external world and myself while I work. As the repulsive and attractive characteristics of work come into balance, it becomes harder to take a stable, definite attitude toward the work at hand.

Somewhere between the realms of pain and pleasure, between the realms of enslaving and liberating work, lies the region of boredom. Occupied with undemanding, routine labor, I grow bored and fall into absentmindedness. Like Ishmael on lookout at the masthead, I lose the sense of the special time and place I live in. The job occupies me without occupying my attention. Unless my fantasies entrance me, time hangs heavy on my hands. My mind does one thing and my hands another. If my fantasies entrance me and the work is dangerous, I risk killing or maiming myself or someone else on the job. I had such an experience when my spear wrenched free of my hands and went hurtling down a factory aisle in the Goodrich tire-building department.

Literary representations of work, descendants of the commentaries on work in myths and proverbs, tend to emphasize work's frightful, degrading, and boring aspects. Dangers to life and limb lurk in the workaday world. The Proverbial sluggard, safe in his bed, imagines that to venture into the world is to risk dismemberment. "There is a lion without, I shall be slain in the streets!" he protests to the housewife who is trying to rouse him (Prov. 22:13). There may be no lion out there, but his apprehensions are far from groundless. Work is doom for Sisyphus in Hades; it is endless and without permanently visible results as it is also for the woman whose work is never done. It may also be a kind of Herculean, purgatorial task, exacted to make the sufferer worthy of admittance to the Elysian Fields.

That work is a curse remains the dominant view; an Eden of easy living, or at most a minimal amount of dressing and keeping of the garden, is counterposed to a slavish fallen world of punishing effort. After the expulsion from the Garden, Adam is sentenced to life at hard labor and Eve is sentenced to patriarchy and labor pains. From there on the normal human condition, according to this interpretation of the myth, is one of continuing economic, social, and biological misery.

Adherents of the doctrine of progress and transcendental optimists reject the doctrine of Original Sin; the first human beings, in their view, did not bequeath inescapable punishment to their descendants. The optimists insist that oppressive labor is not a necessary condition of human life. "It is not necessary, that a man should earn his living by the sweat of his brow, unless he sweats easier than I do."[12]

For Marx and his followers humanity is on the threshold of a world community of peace and plenty in which human needs will be met without the exploitation of labor. Marxian summonses to socialist revolution in the twentieth century have frequently been justified on the assumption of the ripeness of the productive forces for the construction of a classless society. The implication is that the revolutionary project for the emancipation of labor was untimely in previous centuries.

Utopians like Thoreau, by contrast, do not acknowledge historical circumstances that limit the possibilities for radical social change. For them the challenge to drudgery and exploitation might be successfully made at any moment in history. It is always timely to ask why human beings are so docile, always timely to summon them to revolt against a slavish life. The inhabitants of Concord reminded Thoreau, when he considered their ways of making a living, of Hindu ascetics ritually humiliating themselves day by day. Why should this be so? It seemed to Thoreau to be a kind of mistake attributable to a lack of awareness of possible alternatives. Hence his eagerness "to wake my neighbors up," as he proclaims in his self-reliant epigraph to *Walden* (self-reliant because, departing from customary practice in the devising of epigraphs, he quotes himself rather than another author). All slaves can come out of bondage right now; the curse on Adam can be repealed at this instant.

When Thoreau lifts the curse of hard labor from the shoulders of the race and professes faith in the immediate accessibility of an Eden of unalienated humanity, the Eden of his vision is not a paradise of idleness, though it affords plenty of time for contemplation. It is rather a place where people work playfully and play productively; there the line between the serious and the sportive is erased or at least obscured. We are to take it easy in his Eden but are not to be passive consumers of its delights.

Thoreau is among the revolutionary-utopian interpreters of the myth of the Garden. Foremost in that tradition, in the English language, is John Milton. Writing when the capitalist mode of production and its attendant work ethic were changing the world, Milton saw the Fall in the Garden from a point of view uncongenial to the kind of work normal in a fallen world where humanity must endure subordination coerced by violence or the threat of violence. Work, in Milton's account of it in *Paradise Lost,* was originally a slow-paced, amorous dressing and keeping of the Garden. Then unfortunately—it was fortunate only for the Messiah who, without the Fall, would have been out of work, deprived of a mission in history—Eve gives way to guilt feelings about the style, tempo, and consequent low productivity of the work she and Adam perform in the Garden. Eve's onset of guilt about work is a necessary preparation for the temptation and Fall. Eve fears that she and Adam do not do enough work to deserve their food; she wants to feel that they have earned their food. They could earn it by working harder, more productively. They would work more efficiently, she reasons, if they would work in isolation from each other rather than by cooperating as they began working.

The primitive organization of work that Eve guiltily criticizes and proposes to abandon is one in which the pair tend the Garden together, just hard enough to work up an appetite for lunch, just fast enough to raise a light sweat and to appreciate a cooling breeze, not to the point of exhaustion, not enough to ruin their living experience of associated labor. Adam wishes to stick to the original way of working, so Eve and Adam debate how they should work in the Garden. When Eve deplores its inefficiency, Adam defends their original way of working with the argument that human beings are not on earth to fulfill work quotas or test their virtue by enduring separation from one another. He pleads eloquently but is no match for Eve's guilt-ridden determination to boost labor efficiency. So Adam and Eve go to work in different parts of the Garden and inevitably meet the mysterious challenge to human integrity associated with the first division of labor. What they then taste is the voluntary experience of evil. They have succumbed to the demon of efficiency before they taste the forbidden fruit. They then experience orgiastic sensuality and mutual estrangement in rapid succession.[13] These are the first fruits of the cult of efficiency.

So history begins with humanity condemned to a world in which private property, the state, and hard work are necessary consequences of the Fall. The penalties of civilization could have been avoided if only the ancestors of the race had been obedient to the God of freedom. Their disobedience lost us freedom and subjected us to necessity. The powers that be may be ordained of God, but if so, that does not condone the subjugation of humanity to oppressive institutions. Or as Milton puts it: "Tyranny must be / Though to the tyrant no excuse."[14] Milton lived and wrote in the faith that, with superhuman effort, paradise, the lost just commonwealth, will be regained. He calls for struggle "to repair the ruins of our first parents" by learning to know and obey the God of freedom.[15] A person committed to that goal may imitate either the patient witness of the martyr or the violent outbreak against tyranny of the blood avenger; either Christ or Samson; perhaps both.

Hegel, a century and half ago, predicted that American politics would retain a festival character as long as the forest rules the American imagination.[16] Perhaps he was right, though it has not been the festival of the oppressed that Marx imagined when he thought of social revolution. The oppressed have had their roles in the American festival assigned to them by choreographers with intentions other than the emancipation of labor. Yet there is a kind of ritual release from drudgery activated by the powerful forest of the mind. In the forest we return to reason, thought Emerson (*NA*, 692), finding there a vantage point from which to view and judge civilization, a point from which the difference between what is and what might be may be measured, a point from which the criticism of work may help us see better some facets of our many faceted literature.

NOTES

Introduction

1. Most of the quotaions from Thoreau's works are cited in the text using the following abbreviations:

   NA: The Norton Anthology of American Literature, ed. Ronald Gottesman, Laurence B. Holland, David Kalstone, Francis Murphy, Herschel Parker, and William R. Pritchard (New York and London: W. W. Norton & Co., 1979), vol. 1.

   ME: Thoreau: The Major Essays, ed. Jeffrey L. Duncan (New York: E. P. Dutton, 1972).
2. Karl Marx, "Economic and Philosophical Manuscripts," in *The Marx-Engels Reader,* ed. Robert Tucker (New York: W. W. Norton & Co., 1978), pp. 75–76.
3. Marx, "The German Ideology," in Tucker, p. 124.
4. Ibid.
5. *The Complete Poems of Emily Dickinson,* ed. Thomas H. Johnson (Boston and Toronto: Little Brown and Company, 1955).

Chapter 1

1. Edwin I. Moser, "Henry David Thoreau: The College Essays" (M.A. thesis, New York University, 1951), p. 184. In Walter Harding, *A Thoreau Handbook* (New York: New York University Press, 1959), p. 41.

2. *Boston Quarterly Review,* vol. 1 (1835), p. 191.
3. Thoeau, *Journal* (1845–57), 1, in *The Writings of Henry David Thoreau,* ed. Bradford Torrey and Francis Allen (Boston and New York: Houghton Mifflin, 1906), p. 426.
4. *Walden and Other Writings,* ed. Brooks Atkinson (New York: Modern Library, 1950), pp. 677–78.
5. Friedrich Engels, "On Authority," in Tucker, ed., p. 731.
6. *The Communist Manifesto,* in Tucker, ed., p. 491.
7. Karl Marx, *Capital,* vol. 1 (London: Lawrence and Wishart, 1974), p. 174.

Chapter 2

1. *Moby Dick* is a novel of 135 chapters prefaced by "Etymology" and "Extracts" and followed by a one-page "Epilogue." The length of the average chapter is five to six pages. There are plenty of usable editions. Readers wishing to check the context of my citations from the novel would be best served if I cite only the chapter, omitting page references to a particular edition, with this first and all following references.

Chapter 3

1. The following details of Dickinson family history in their social context are drawn from Richard B. Sewall, *The Life of Emily Dickinson* (New York: Farrar, Straus and Giroux, 1974), 2 vols., and from Nancy Harris Brose, Juliana McGovern Dupre, Wendy Tocher Kohler, and Jean McClure Mudge, *Emily Dickinson: Profile of the Poet as Cook, with Selected Recipes* (Amherst, Mass.: Hamilton I. Newell, Inc., 1976).
2. Brose et al., p. 6.
3. Jean McClure Mudge, *Emily Dickinson and the Image of Home* (Amherst: The University of Massachusetts Press, 1975), p. 84.
4. Edward Taylor, "The Preface," *God's Determinations Touching His Elect,* p. 1.4.
5. Johnson, ed. "Burglar! Banker-Father!" is the penultimate line of Poem 49, in the Johnson enumeration. Further citations of Dickinson poems will be parenthical in the text, by Johnson number.

6. Sewall, pp. 145, 130, xxii.
7. Brose et al., p. 6.
8. Taylor, 11.9–12. The degradation of work through the division of labor is not in the world Taylor represents in *God's Determinations Touching the Elect.* Taylor's Creative Worker uses carpentry, metallurgy and foundry work, stonemasonary, and housewifery. Taylor's God is no drudging specialist but truly a master of all trades. Dickinson in Poem 231 imagines God as a production manager who lets angels out to play in the afternoons if they have met their daily work quota. Between the seventeenth and nineteenth centuries God declined from a master craftsman into a mere supervisor, if the witness of Taylor and Dickinson can be credited.
9. Brose et al., p. 6.

Chapter 4

1. Samuel Johnson, *Taxation No Tyranny,* cited in *The Oxford Dictionary of Quotations,* 2d ed. (1953, rev. 1959) (London: Oxford University Press, 1959), p. 278:26.
2. *Narrative of the Life of Frederick Douglass, an American Slave. Written by Himself* (New York: New American Library, 1968), pp. 31–32; subsequent citations are parentheitcal.

Chapter 5

1. Walt Whitman, *Leaves of Grass: Comprehensive Reader's Edition,* ed. Harold W. Blodgett and Scully Bradley (New York: New York University Press, 1965). The two portraits are the second and third of the group bound between pp. 516–17 of this edition. The editors note that Bucke dates the photograph from 1856 and not 1849 as Whitman himself does. Which if either date is correct is not vital here; the point is that the poet presented two widely different images of himself to the world during the years of his greatest creativity. The relevant words from Emerson's letter of acknowledgment to Whitman (appended to this edition of *Leaves of Grass,* pp. 229–30) are "I greet

you at the beginning of a great career, which yet must have had a long foreground somewhere, for such a start. I rubbed my eyes a little, to see if this sunbeam were no illusion; but the solid sense of the book is a sober certainty. . . . I did not know until I last night saw the book advertised in a newspaper that I could trust the name as real and available for a post-office."

2. This and subsequent citations from *Leaves of Grass* are by poem title preceding the quotation(s) and section and line number(s) following; e.g., "Song of Myself" (section) 1 (line) 5; (section) 11 (lines) 35–40. If the entire poem is quoted, no line numbers are given.
3. Dickinson, "His feet are shod with gauze—," in Johnson, ed., 19. This is Poem 906 in Johnson's enumeration.
4. "To the States, To Identify the 16th, 17th or 18th Presidentiad," 1.4. In this poem Whitman asks himself how, in the mounting crisis over slavery, he could be prone and "all drowsing." Revulsion at the American political situation provides him an answer: "What a filthy Presidentiad! . . . / Are those really Congressmen? are those the great Judges? The proslavery performance of the presidents, the Congress, and the Supreme Court between the Compromise of 1850 and the Dred Scott decision is what he responds to. What he sees gives him an excuse for political passivity, for the time being: Then I will sleep awhile yet, for I see that these States / sleep, for reasons. . . . (11.5–6)
5. "Preface 1855," p. 720. Blodgett and Bradley call "Song of the Exposition" "one of WW's comparative failures because it does not surmount its own rhetoric" (p. 196). There is much embarrassing messianic chauvinism in the poem. Before the Civil War, when in better control of his patriotism, Whitman writes in an aside in "Song of the Broad-Axe" "(America! I do not vaunt my love for you, / I have what I have.)"(11.184–85)
6. Blodgett and Bradley, p. 189, footnote to "Song of the Broad-Axe, 1.108.

Conclusion

1. Joe Glazer, "The Mill Was Made of Marble," in John Greenway, *American Folksongs of Protest* (Philadelphia: University of Pennsylvania, 1953), p. 9.
2. *Walden,* "Economy," Gottesman et al., p. 1547.

3. Ruth McKenney, *Industrial Valley* (New York: Greenwood Press, 1968), p. 302 (reprint of Curtis, Brown Ltd., 1939).
4. Ibid., p. 362.
5. Ibid., p. 366.
6. Ibid., p. 367.
7. Xenophon, *Oeconomicus,* 4 (2, 3), quoted in Melvin Kranzberg and Joseph Gies, *By the Sweat of Thy Brow: Work in the Western World* (New York: G. P. Putnam's Sons, 1975), p. 27.
8. Milton, *Paradise Lost,* 7, lines 485–87.
9. Whitman, *Song of Myself,* 1.76.
10. Ibid., 1.684.
11. *Walden,* p. 1601.
12. *Walden,* "Economy," p. 1575.
13. *Paradise Lost,* 9, 11.205–1188.
14. *Paradise Lost,* 12, 11.95–96.
15. Milton, "Of Education," in Frank Allen Patterson, ed., *The Student's Milton: Being the Complete Poems of John Milton with the Greater Part of His Prose Works, Now Printed in One Volume, Together with New Translations into English of His Italian, Latin, and Greek Poems,* rev. ed. (New York: Appleton-Century-Crofts, Inc., 1933), p. 726.
16. G. W. F. Hegel, *Vorlesungen die Philosophie der Geschichte, Saemtliche Werke,* ed. Hermann Glockner (Stuttgart, 1928), vol. 11, p. 129.

BIBLIOGRAPHY

Boston Quarterly Reivew 1 (1835).

Brose, Nancy Harris, Juliana McGovern Dupre, Wendy Tocher Kohler, and Jean McClure Mudge. *Emily Dickinson: Profile of the Poet as Cook, with Selected Recipes.* Amherst, Mass.: Hamilton I. Newell, Inc., 1976.

Dickinson, Emily. *The Complete Poems of Emily Dickinson.* Edited by Thomas H. Johnson. Boston and Toronto: Little Brown and Company, 1955.

Douglass, Frederick. *Narrative of the Life of Frederick Douglass, an American Slave, Written by Himself.* New York: New American Library, 1968.

Emerson, Ralph Waldo. *The Norton Anthology of American Literature.* Edited by Ronald Gottesman, Laurence B. Holland, David Kalstone, Francis Murphy, Hershel Parker, and William R. Pritchard. New York and London: W. W. Norton and Company, 1979. Includes *The American Scholar* and *Nature.*

Greenway, John. *American Folksongs of Protest.* Philadelphia: University of Pennsylvania, 1953. Includes Glazer's "The Mill Was Made of Marble."

Harding, Walter. *A Thoreau Handbook.* New York: New York University Press, 1959.

Hegel, G. W. F. *Vorlesungen die Philosophie der Geschichte, Saemtliche Werke.* Edited by Hermann Glockner. Stuttgart, 1928. Vol. 11.

Kranzberg, Melvin, and Joseph Gies. *By the Sweat of Thy Brow: Work in the Western World.* New York: G. P. Putnam's Sons, 1975.

McKenney, Ruth. *Industrial Valley.* New York: Greenwood Press, 1968 (reprint of Curtis, Brown Ltd., 1939).

Marx, Karl. *Capital.* Vol. 1. London: Lawrence and Wishart, 1974.

———. *The Marx-Engels Reader.* Edited by Robert C. Tucker. New York: W. W. Norton and Company, 1978. Includes "Economic and Philosophical Manuscripts," "The German Ideology," and *The Communist Manifesto.*

Milton, John. *Paradise Lost.*

———. *The Student's Milton: Being the Complete Poems of John Milton with the Greater Part of His Prose Works, Now Printed in One Volume, Together with New Translations into English of His Italian, Latin, and Greek Poems.* New York: Appleton-Century-Crofts, Inc., 1933.

Moser, Edwin I. "Henry David Thoreau: The College Essays." Master's thesis, New York University, 1951.

Mudge, Jean McClure. *Emily Dickinson and the Image of Home.* Amherst: The Univesity of Massachusetts Press, 1975.

Sewall, Richard B. *The Life of Emily Dickinson.* New York: Farrar, Straus and Giroux, 1974. 2 vols.

Taylor, Edward. *The Norton Anthology of American Literature.* Edited by Ronald Gottesman, Laurence B. Holland, David Kalstone, Francis Murphy, Hershel Parker, and William R. Pritchard. New York and London: W. W. Norton and Company, 1979. Includes "The Preface" to *God's Determinations Touching His Elect.*

Thoreau, Henry David. *The Norton Anthology of American Literature.* Edited by Ronald Gottesman, Laurence B. Holland, David Kalstone, Francis Murphy, Hershel Parker, and William R. Pritchard. New York and London: W. W. Norton and Company, 1979. Includes *Walden.*

———. *Thoreau: The Major Essays.* Edited by Jeffrey L. Duncan. New York: E. P. Dutton, 1972. Includes *Thomas Carlyle and His Works* and *Paradise (To Be) Regained.*

———. *Walden and Other Writings.* Edited by Brooks Atkinson. New York: Modern Library, 1950.

———. *The Writings of Henry David Thoreau.* Edited by Bradford Torrey and Francis Allen. Boston and New York: Houghton Mifflin, 1906. Includes *Journal* (1845–57).

Whitman, Walt. *Leaves of Grass: Comprehensive Reader's Edition.* Edited by Harold W. Blodgett and Scully Bradley. New York: New York University Press, 1965.

INDEX